BATTENBERG AND POINT LAC[

by Nellie Clarke Brown

edited by Jules & Kaethe Kliot

INTRODUCTION

The name BATTENBERG LACE has been applied to a form of needle lace only since the early 1890's. The earlier forms of this lace however, date back to the 16th century when it was referred to as *Mezzo Punto*. In modern times names such as *Renaissance Lace, Branscomb Point, Tape Lace, Milanese lace, Irish lace, Belgium lace* and *"Real Lace"* have been used to describe this technique.

The essential element of the technique is the pre-made tape which outlines and follows the main lines of the design. The voids left are then filled with any variety of needle lace stitches using only a needle and thread. The procedure is simple and familiar to anyone with skills in any of the needle related crafts. Battenberg lace captures much of the charm of the traditional needle laces and yet permits the expediency demanded of the contemporary lace maker.

In recent years, Battenberg Lace has taken on new dimensions as the basic technique has been adapted to machine embroidery. Using a "dissolving stabilizer" as the base material, the tape is machine sewn directly to this base. Infilling stitches can be made by sewing through the stabilizer or by cutting away the stabilizer in select areas where free stitches are desired. Other voids can be filled by simply sewing any finished material, such as lace yardage to the tape perimeter of these voids and then trimming the excess away. The base is then completely removed by dampening with water. There are several books listed in the bibliography which give more detailed instructions for machine lace techniques.

While this book is designed for the maker of hand laces, the lace and stitch patterns will be of considerable value to the machine lace maker.

BATTENBERG AND POINT LACE BOOK is a republication of the "PRISCILLA BATTENBERG AND POINT LACE BOOK" by Nellie Clarke Brown, 1912, Priscilla Publishing Company. Published near the end of the great Battenberg era, this book is a compilation of many of the earlier books including the 1892 edition of the Florence Home Needlework (where the technique was referred to as Irish Lace), and, to our knowledge, is the most complete. An appendix follows illustrating a group of designs published in 1900. Any of these designs can be ordered full size from this publisher, or they can be a source for ideas for your own designs.

Typical of books of this period, most references to materials and supplies as well as prices are no longer relevant and so the following working notes are provided. Consideration is given to both hand and machine techniques.

WORKING NOTES

PREPARING PATTERNS

The working pattern is a full size layout of the project or portion of the project (if of repeat designs such as a border). Traditionally, a tinted, glazed cotton was used on which the pattern was printed or transferred. A smooth polished cotton is still the ideal material, especially if it is to be used more then once. If you have a heat transfer pattern it can be transferred directly to such a material

with an ordinary iron set on high temperature (linen). The more traditional method of transferring a pattern is to "prick" a series of pin holes along all the lines of the paper over a firm soft material such a insulating wall board, and using a pricker with a needle, making holes approximately 1/8" apart. A pricking wheel (pins set into a round disk) can speed up this process considerably. When the pricking is complete, the paper pattern is laid over the cloth on which you will work, and dusted with a fine powder using a pounce, which passes through the holes marking the cloth below. An unlimited number of transfers can be made with this method. For one time use, a paper pattern can be used directly. A white butcher paper can also be an excellent pattern material. It typically has a plastic or wax coating on one side and paper on the other. The white paper is usually transparent enough to trace through. Carbon paper should generally be avoided as it can stain the finished work. Another technique for transferring patterns is via a photocopy. A photocopy pattern can often be transferred by means of a hot iron.

For machine lace work the ideal pattern material is referred to as "dissolving stabilizer". It is a plastic like material which completely disappears when dampened with water and is translucent so you can trace directly over a printed pattern using a felt pen.

WORKING TAPE

After a complete disappearance of tapes for many years, there are now on the market a wide selection of tapes, generally falling into three styles.

The **BELGIUM TAPES** are currently the most popular and are a delight to use as they are easily contoured to the tightest curves. These modern "pull braids" are bias woven and incorporate a pull thread on each edge, which, when pulled, causes the tape to form a smooth curve. These tapes come in a variety of widths and designs, some incorporating a heavy gimp thread, giving it a dimensional look. Many of the tapes are also available with a picot edge along one side, suitable for the outer edge of a piece.

The **FRENCH TAPES** are straight woven in the traditional Battenberg lace style and generally requires folding to manipulate curves, although some contouring is possible. These tapes typically have a solid center and small holes along each edge. They are available in several widths.

NOVELTY TAPES are also available and are used generally in combination with the plain tapes. These are of undulating designs and are sometimes referred to a "Honiton" or "princess" tapes as they were traditionally used to simulate the leaf designs of handmade Honiton lacer and Modern Brussels lace. Some are very delicate and others relatively heavy.

It should be noted that tapes can also be made by hand. A bobbin lace tape can be easily made with few bobbins and in any variety of designs. These would be similar to the French tapes in appearance. A crocheted chain can be made as good alternative to a machine made tape. Hairpin lace techniques using a crochet fork and hook provide another alternative to the machine tape.

To use the Belgium tapes, start by basting the tape to your pattern. Always baste along the edge that is on the outer side of any curve. If the curve reverses, move the basting stitch to the corresponding outer edge of the curve. If done correctly the tape will bulge up on the inner edge of the curve. If you have trouble handling the tape, it can be pinned in place prior to basting. After working approximately every 6 to 12 inches of tape or before making any folds in the tape, pull the "edge" thread, from the tape end, causing the tape to lie flat. The "edge" thread runs just inside the edge and parallel to the edge and is a stiffer thread from the rest. It is a good idea to find this thread and practice pulling it prior to starting work. If longer lengths are used, the "pull" thread will generally need to be pulled through at points within the tape length, preferably at a location where the tape is folded. When you have found this thread pull it out from the tape forming a loop. A small loop can be twisted and easily concealed. If the loop becomes large, simply cut it in the center and tie the two ends together with a square knot, cutting off the extending threads. For sharp turns, fold the tape in the normal manner as the tape is identical on both sides.

FILLINGS

The fillings can be any of the variety of types found in this book or any variation of these as one might discover. Fillings, however can also be of a decorative fabric such as velvet, satin or lace yardage and it can even be combined with needlework stitches or needlework stitches can be worked directly over them. When using fabric fillings always cut the fabric after the tape is securely stitched to it. Stitching can be done by hand or by machine. Those style of tape lace can be compared to leaded glass, where the tape reflects to lead work and the fabric the glass. A tape of a more solid design will be found most suitable for this style of working.

APPLIQUE

The tape can be appliqued to a cotton tulle, avoiding the need for any infilling stitches. Commonly known as "Princess Lace" this style typically used the novelty braids, closely simulating the hand made bobbin laces.

CENTERS

Many designs for doilies, handkerchiefs, etc. require a solid center. Linen or cotton batiste is suggested for the smaller pieces and a heavier linen for table linens and larger pieces.

RINGS

Rings are incorporated into many of the designs. These are made by wrapping the thread around a ring gauge as described in the body of this text or around your finger and then solidly buttonholing over with buttonhole stitches. Rings can also be crocheted or tatted or bone rings can be used and covered with buttonhole stitches. Tatted rings can incorporate small or large picots to which the tape can be secured. Rings should be made prior to the start of the work.

THREAD

Threads for the filling stitches can be of whatever material, size or color that suits the lace maker. Most of the contemporary Belgium Lace of this style uses a relatively heavy thread such as a #5 pearl cotton. For the more traditional working, DMC Cordonnet is recommended in sizes 30, 40, or 50, the higher the number the finer the thread. It is suggested that a small sample of the stitch to be used be made prior to the actual work.

For the initial basting of the tape, an ordinary sewing thread of any contrasting color is suggested.

NEEDLES

Two needles are suggested, the size depending on the threads used. A #9 sharp is suitable for the basting work while a blunt pointed tapestry needle is suggested for working the stitches. For the finer threads a #24 is suggested while a relatively larger size would be required if using heavier infilling threads.

PATTERNS

There are currently many sources for Battenberg patterns ranging from reprints of the traditional patterns to new designs specifically suited to the contemporary Belgium tapes. Patterns as illustrated in this book can be photographically enlarged or manually copied by graphing, or can be ordered full size. If the analogy between Battenberg Lace and stained glass is understood, you can find many ideas in stained glass pattern books, the tape substituted for the lead work.

CARE AND CLEANING

The standard Battenberg tapes are hard finished cotton and can be cleaned with mild soap and water. A little starch in the rinse water will restore the crispness of the original piece. If cleaning an old piece of lace, starch should be avoided, and agitation minimized during the wash and rinse cycle. The lace should be laid flat to dry as hanging will distort the work, and the weight is likely to weaken if not break the infilling threads. If possible, dry the lace on a sheet of glass. Lace dried in this way will require minimum ironing

BIBLIOGRAPHY

HAND TECHNIQUE

NEEDLE LACES: BATTENBERG, POINT & RETICELLA, Kliot
NEEDLE LACES AND NET EMBROIDERIES, Preston
BATTENBERG AND OTHER TAPE LACE, Butterick
NEEDLE-MADE LACE, Earnshaw
PIZZO RINASCIMENTO, Mani di Fata

MACHINE TECHNIQUE

HOW TO MAKE NEEDLE LACE ON YOUR SEWING MACHINE, Gail Kibiger
MACHINE EMBROIDERY, McNeill
KALOCSAI GEPHIMZES (Hungarian machine lace)

DESIGNS

LE TENDE (Curtain Designs)

SOURCE OF SUPPLY

LACIS, 2982 Adeline St., Berkeley, CA 94703. Wide variety of tapes, threads, patterns and books. Send $1.00 for catalog covering Battenberg Lace and all other lace techniques.

LACIS
PUBLICATIONS

3163 Adeline Street, Berkeley, CA 94703

© 1986, Lacis
Second Edition, © 1987, Lacis
Third Edition, ©1989, Lacis
ISBN 0-916896-26-9

How to Make Battenberg and Point Lace.

Selection of Materials.

HE same rules and instruction apply to Battenberg and modern point lace. The latter, being much the finer and more delicate, requires more time and patience. Both deserve equal care.

Braid and Thread.

The pattern being chosen, select a smooth linen braid. Great care should be taken to avoid getting a cotton braid. The beauty and value of many a piece of Battenberg lace has been lessened because it was made with a cotton braid.

The working thread, as well as all other parts of the work, should always be linen. There are various lace threads that are good, and each has its friends. Some of the threads that are so slightly twisted as to resemble floss are good for the filling of rings, and, when a soft, indefinite effect is desired, is the right thing for their covering of buttonhole stitch or crochet. When it is desired to have each thread in the covering of the ring stand out distinctly, thread more tightly twisted should be used. For overcasting the braid, Nos. 70 or 80 may be used, while for the filling-in stitches, Nos. 40 to 60 should be selected, according to the degree of fineness desired in the work. The narrow braid calls for a finer thread than the wider braid requires. None of the cotton threads should be used for any part of the permanent work. To avoid knots and tangles in the working thread, the needle should always be threaded from the right end of the thread, and before working the thread should be drawn through the thumb and finger of the left hand to lessen its liability to twist and tangle.

For needle point lace the best thread is the "Petit Moulin" linen lace thread, manufactured for the purpose in France. This thread may be had in numbers from 30 to 1500. For the very finest lace, Nos. 1000 to 1500 should be used, while for doilies and handkerchiefs it is advisable to use a slightly heavier thread. Nos. 600 to 1000 are good. In making Honiton and princess lace, Nos. 100 to 600 are most effective. The coarser threads are excellent for Battenberg lace.

This thread comes in balls, varying in size from the tiny ball of No. 1500 to the large ball of No. 30. Around the outside is pasted a ring of stiff paper, which serves as a protector for the thread, and keeps it free from soil. This paper should not be removed, but the thread should be used from the centre of the ball. On one side of the ball is a thread passing across from the centre to the circumference. By pulling this thread an end is discovered, and the ball unwinds from the inside in the fashion of most balls of thread and twine. It is advisable to put the ball into a little box, through a puncture in the lid of which the thread may be drawn without risk of soil or injury. Thread bags of various kinds may be used instead of the box.

Rings.

Very excellent rings may be bought ready for use, but many ladies prefer to make them. For their use a very handy little ring gauge has been invented, and is shown in miniature in Fig. 1.

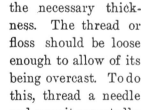

This provides for the making of rings in six different sizes, and permits of their being made of any thickness desired. The thread or floss is wound around the chosen section of the ring gauge a sufficient number of times, perhaps twenty, to make the ring of the necessary thickness. The thread or floss should be loose enough to allow of its being overcast. To do this, thread a needle

FIG. 1. RING GAUGE AND BUTTON-HOLED RING FOR BATTENBERG AND POINT LACE.

and pass it repeatedly around the roll of threads by pushing the needle between the threads and the ring gauge. When it is closely overcast, push the thread ring carefully off the ring gauge without marring its circular shape. To do this successfully, give it a series of little pushes with the thumb around and around its circumference until it slips off. It is now a ring of threads held in place by the overcasting thread which is coiled around it. It may now be finished in either one or two ways. It may be covered with a close row of buttonhole stitches, and so resemble the ready-made ring, or it may be covered with a close row of single crochet. The end may be fastened by passing it through the threads of the ring. If the needle is thrust through the body of the ring, and carries the thread a short distance from the finishing place, and then with another stitch returns to its starting-point, the end will be safely secured. To make the rings exactly alike, care should be taken to have the thread circle the ring gauge exactly the same number of times in each ring.

Rings for the needle point lace should be very slender and delicate. The thread should be wound around the gauge from four to eight or ten times, then overcast and buttonholed. Crochet is not practical for these dainty rings. When a substitute for the ring gauge is desired, bone knitting-needles, pencils, or tiny glass bottles may be used.

Basting and Overcasting.

THE first work is basting the braid to the pattern. In most patterns the braid is represented by a double line. In basting, one edge of the braid should follow the outer line of the pattern, and the basting threads should be placed through the open edge of the braid and upon the outer line of the pattern designating the braid. When the progress of the pattern changes the outer line or curve, to which you have been basting, to the inner curve, the basting thread should be carried across the braid as is shown in the illustration (Fig. 2), and the basting continued along what is now the outer curve.

FIG. 2. METHOD OF BASTING BRAID IN BATTENBERG AND POINT LACE.

The basting stitches should be rather close and short, and should be drawn tightly so as to hold the braid firmly to its place. Should the basting stitches be loose, the putting in of the lace stitches will inevitably draw the braid from its place on the pattern and spoil the perfection of the lines and curves of the design.

Back stitching is neither necessary nor advisable. The forward stitches taken closely and firmly will hold the braid securely, and are easy to remove. Braid that is back stitched to the pattern makes an unnecessarily tedious task of the separating of the work from the pattern just at the time when the completion of the stitches makes the worker unusually eager to see the work completed.

Never under any circumstances should any but a straight length of braid be basted through the middle. Should the braid be basted through the middle when following a curve, it is almost impossible not to draw it too tight, and as a result the outer edge will curl up and utterly spoil the work, as no amount of care in placing the stitches can make right a piece of work where the outer edge of the braid around a curve rises in its might, and reaches longingly towards its opposite and inner edge.

Turning Corners.

Great care should be observed in turning corners, and various methods are employed for corners of different angles. In an obtuse corner (Fig. 3, *a*), or one so broad and shallow as to be almost a curve, it is only necessary to follow the outer curve of the pattern of the braid, and allow the resulting fulness to remain loose until the overcasting stitches draw it down into shape.

In sharp or acute angles (Fig. 3, *b*) the braid may be basted to the extreme point of the angle, and the fulness folded over, so the fold will lie along the edge of the braid, as the basting is continued along the second side of the point.

In a sharp angle the fold of the braid may also be turned under (Fig. 3, *c*), the fold being so regulated that its ends reach from the exact point of the outer edge of the braid or pattern to the exact point of the inner edge. This forms a mitered corner and divides the point exactly in halves.

Still another way (Fig. 3, *d*) is applicable to an angle of any degree, but it cuts off the end of the point. In this method, when the point is approached, the braid is simply turned over upon itself at the angle necessary to allow the braid upon either side of the fold to follow the line of the design.

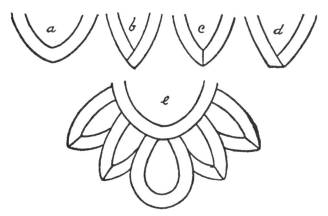

FIG. 3. METHOD OF BASTING BATTENBERG AND POINT LACE BRAID ON CORNERS AND CURVES.

In all cases the point of the braid should be securely fastened to the pattern in such a way that its end will not stand out from the pattern and form a hook or projection, around which the working thread will be prone to catch at the risk of pricked fingers, tangled thread, and stitches dragged out of shape. A stitch or two carried from the point of the braid to the pattern beyond will hold all points securely and will repay the care expended many times. Hurried basting, with loose points and corners, often results in great loss of time and perfection of work.

Scallops and Loops.

Where the pattern contains a series of overlapping scallops or loops, with one width of braid between them (Fig. 3, *e*), the braid should not be cut but doubled back upon itself. Baste the braid upon the outer edge of the design until it reaches the braid that checks its course. Turn it back upon itself so that the fold just touches the other braid and may be overcast to it. Let the edge of the returning braid follow the outer line of the pattern of the next scallop or loop.

Where the design of the pattern contains a series of scallops or loops on either side of a central figure (Fig. 3, *e*) the braid may be put on with the foldings in the order in which they come, but this destroys the similarity of the two sides. A better appearance is obtained by having the two sides similar. In turning the braid back upon itself at the end or top of the loop, it is brought *over* the already basted braid of the preceding loop. On the opposite side it is best to turn the braid *under* the side of the preceding loop. This must be done before the basting of the preceding loop is completed.

Upon reaching the point where the two braids diverge, the end of the braid nearest the bastings is taken in the fingers of the left hand, and with the fingers of the right hand is doubled back or under that held in the left hand. Lay the doubled braid down upon the pattern, being sure that it is just sufficiently long to reach the end of the loop or scallop. One row of basting fastens the two layers of braid into place. It is best to cut the braid as seldom as possible, and this method of turning back the braid saves many cuttings, and presents a much neater appearance than when it is cut at every opportunity.

Overcasting.

After the braid has all been carefully basted into place, the full inner edges of the curves must also be brought into place. To do this they must be overcast with a very fine linen thread. This overcasting thread should pass over and over the edge of the braid and into each of its marginal loops. Only occasionally, on very large, slightly curved lines, may a loop be here and there omitted.

On the edges of spaces to be filled with twisted bars, spiders, wheels, and other similar stitches where the working thread must pass from point to point along the edge of the braid, the overcasting may be omitted, and the passage of the working thread utilized to draw the braid into place as it proceeds in its course of completing the stitch. Familiarity with the work will show when the work of overcasting may in this way be lessened. The overcasting thread should not be drawn tight enough to draw the braid from its place on the pattern, but it should be tight enough to hold the inner gathered edge smoothly down to the pattern, where it must fit as flatly as its opposite outer edge.

Whenever the overcasting thread reaches a place where two edges of the braid meet or cross, the needle should be passed through both braids, either in a simple overcasting stitch or with a single buttonhole knot. When the thread passes from one side to the other of two braid edges the thread should connect them at both sides.

When in the course of the overcasting the curve of the braid changes, and the inner curve becomes the outer one, a buttonhole stitch should be taken in the edge of the braid at the point where the curve changes and the thread carefully woven through the braid to its opposite side, where another buttonhole stitch should be taken and the overcasting continued.

Cutting the Braid.

Where the ends of a braid meet at a corner, or other place having no other braid to hide the juncture, fold the end of the *under* braid *up* and the end of the *upper* braid *down*, and lay the one upon the other. Overcast them together at the end of both braids. The beginning of the basting of the braid to the design, as well as the joining of two ends, should occur at the crossing of two braids. Pass the second braid over the end of the first, and when you again reach that point in the design put the second end under the overlying braid with the first. This makes the upper side the right side.

If it is desired to have the under side of the work, or the side next the pattern, the right side, the manner of procedure should be reversed, and the two ends placed *over* the other braid. These ends should be either turned over and hemmed down neatly, or very carefully overcast to the other braid, that no ragged edges may be seen on either side. The folding over of the ends makes the work a little thicker just at that point, and is more easily noticed than the other finish, which, if carefully done, is hardly visible, and is especially fitted for the finer laces.

Basting the Rings to the Pattern.

When basting on the rings it is well to remember that the basting threads have to be removed later. Only enough are needed to hold the ring in place. If the needle is thrust through the ring four times, twice downwards and twice upwards, it is sufficient. As the rings are not exactly alike on both sides, it is necessary, when placing them, to be very careful to see that the same side is always uppermost. Very pretty effects are obtained by graduating the size of the rings in a row or series. The centre ring may be the largest, and those on either side may decrease in size as they approach the end or point of the space allotted to them, or a large ring may lead a row of others of decreasing size.

When the pattern requires the rings to be placed so close together that they touch, they should be united by threads entering each ring at one point only, and these uniting threads should not be drawn tight enough to bring the rings firmly together, but should serve as a hinge, which, while it keeps the rings together, allows them to move freely. Rings should, under no circumstances, be sewed together along their circumferences, as the effect is stiff and clumsy, and not at all dainty and lace-like.

It is best to baste the rings to the pattern only as the progress of the work requires. The working thread is very apt to catch between the basted rings and the pattern, and so delay the work. After the work of attaching the rings to the braid with the lace stitches has been completed, it is impossible for the thread to catch in this manner.

Fastening the Thread.

Knots should never appear in any lace, and the worker should aim to have both sides of the work appear equally neat and perfect. When the completion of a stitch or the limit of a thread permits the fastening to be made at the intersection of two braids, a single buttonhole knot should be made, and the thread passed, by means of the needle, back and forth, two or three times between the braids with a tiny backstitch at each change of the direction of the thread. When a new thread is to be fastened at the intersection of two braids, the needle should be passed between these two braids with the point toward the place at which the thread is to be fastened. The thread should then be carefully drawn through until the end just disappears from sight between the braids. A buttonhole knot should then be made, and back of it a second one to guard its predecessor.

When, in the course of the work, the end of a used thread must be fastened to a single braid, it may be overcast along the edge of the braid with an occasional buttonhole knot, or a single buttonhole knot may tie the thread to the edge of the braid, and the needle may then pass in a series of tiny running stitches, with an occasional back stitch, along the body of the braid for a short distance. The new thread should then be carried by the needle in a similar manner along the braid from the direction opposite that taken by the retiring thread. At the point where the thread is to be fastened, and the work continued, two button-hole knots are all that is necessary.

It is often well, when filling in with stitches that permit, to begin the new thread on the side of the space opposite the ending of the former thread. This serves to make the place of juncture still less conspicuous.

All patterns should be able to be considered as composed of two parts — design and background. The design should be prominently brought out, and, to accomplish this, the network and other showy stitches should be used, keeping the spider-webs, bars, and other open stitches for the background. It is well to put in the background. stitches first, as they will hold the curves of the braid in place, and preserve the shape of the design until the work is finished.

When working, either side of the lace may be considered the right side. Each has its advantages and disadvantages. The aim of the worker should always be to make both sides so neatly and carefully that they are equally beautiful, and there is no wrong side. Ribbed wheels and some other stitches cannot so easily be worked on the wrong side, and some other stitches appear better on the side upon which they have been worked. Other stitches appear alike on both sides. The overcasting of two braids together, and the beginning and ending of each thread, often appear more plainly upon the upper side and mar the effect of the work, but with care that can be avoided. When the wrong side is up, care must be exercised in placing the rings, which must also be wrong side up. If there is any fear of soiling the work, it is always advisable to make it wrong side up. The under side is usually smoother, but the pressing of the piece when finished makes both sides equally smooth and handsome.

Preparing a Sampler.

 VERY lace-maker should prepare a sampler upon which to reproduce the various lace stitches, which may be worked, cut out, and repeated until proficiency is acquired, and this without danger of soiling or in any way spoiling the piece of work in which the stitch is to be introduced. If every stitch is practised in this way the worker will in the end, besides having become very familiar with the various stitches, have them illustrated in a compact, practical form. Only those workers who have prepared them for use know the comfort and satisfaction to be had in the possession of a sampler.

To prepare this sampler an oblong piece of cambric or holland is required. The size of this depends upon the size of the collection of stitches the worker hopes to obtain, and a sampler is a great incentive to new stitches. What the kodak book and the stamp album are to their devotees, so is the sampler to the lace-worker. A new stitch becomes a great prize and is eagerly added to the collection. In view of this, and that there are over a hundred stitches in common use, it is well to make the sampler sufficiently large.

When holland — the smooth, shiny holland — is used, no additional background is needed. When cambric is used, it is necessary to line it with a sheet of strong but not too stiff paper, or a light weight canvas. With narrow ape or Battenberg braid a part of this sampler is checked off in one-inch squares and the remainder in oblongs one inch by one-half inch in size, as shown in Fig. 4. The squares are for the networks and wheels, while the oblongs are for insertions and bars. The

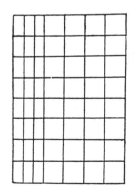

braid presents a very neat appearance, and is delightfully firm if it is first basted in place and then stitched through the centre on the machine. The last piece of braid to be attached should be the one that passes around the others like a frame and covers up the cut ends of the braid. Or a sampler may be made on an all-over lace pattern; this would

FIG. 4. DIAGRAM OF SAMPLER FOR LACE STITCHES.

show the best application of the different stitches to the various shaped spaces.

Lace Stitches. Bars.

LACE stitches may be classified as bars, wheels, insertions, and networks. The first two are used in filling in the background of designs, while the insertions and networks are reserved for the filling in of the design itself.

Sorrento Bars.

The plain twisted bar, Fig. 5, also called the Sorrento bar, is the simplest of all stitches. The thread is fastened securely in the proper place and

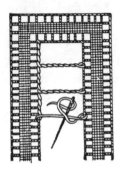

FIG. 5. PLAIN TWISTED BAR.

carried across the space to be filled, where it is held smoothly over the pattern and again secured either by passing it through the edge of the braid or fastening it with a buttonhole knot. The work is then held so that the first fastening of the thread is away from the worker and the second attaching is nearer. The needle is then repeatedly passed under the bar, and the working thread drawn tightly each time, until the opposite end of the bar is reached.

The overcasting away from instead of toward the worker secures a better twist or rope effect, and each twisting or overcasting of the thread helps to keep the preceding overcastings in place, and avoids the loop in the nearer end of the bar, where the thread turns back upon itself.

The working thread is carried from one completed bar to the point from which another is begun by a series of overcasting stitches along the selvage of the braid.

The double twisted bar, Fig. 6, is formed by casting three threads across the space to be filled.

FIG. 6 DOUBLE TWISTED BAR

These threads are stretched just sufficiently to cause them to lie in a straight line between the braids without pulling them from their places. They are then overcast together in an open effect that allows the foundation threads to show between the coiling of the overcasting thread, which winds around them like a tendril.

These bars may be arranged according to fancy, and are grouped in clusters of three, arranged in points and in rays from a common centre, or are placed in parallel lines, when they are sometimes tied through the centre with a series of buttonhole knots, and this tying thread overcast as are the bars.

Plain Buttonhole Bar.

When a bar heavier than the twisted bars is desired, the plain buttonhole bar may be used, as in Fig. 7. The thread is fastened securely and carried across the space to be filled two, three, or four times, according to the weight or size of the

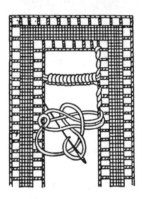

FIG. 7. PLAIN BUTTON-HOLE BAR.

bar desired. The working thread is then carried one loop of the braid-edge lower than the one into which the foundation threads are placed, and the entire bar filled closely and smoothly with a row of buttonhole stitches, which may be worked either from left to right, or from right to left; but the former is the easier, as the thread does not have to be thrown around into position, but falls in place with the working of each stitch. The carrying of the working thread one loop of the braid-edge below the foundation threads of the bar keeps the finished bar in place, and avoids all tendency to curl or twist out of shape. For the same reason, when the end of the bar is reached, the thread is fastened just below the last stitch. Where a series of bars is to be worked, the working thread is overcast along the braid-edge to the desired position of the second bar, and the process repeated. These buttonhole bars may be grouped in various ways, and are often called Point de Venise bars.

Buttonholed Bars with Pinned Picots.

When open picots (also called dots or purls) are desired on the buttonholed bar, they are formed as the work proceeds, at intervals of halves, thirds, quarters, or according to whatever arrangement is chosen. See Fig. 8. A small pin is thrust into the pattern at a distance from the bar corresponding with the desired length of the picot. The working thread is passed under the pin, and is carried over and behind the foundation threads, and outside of the loop held down by the pin. The needle is then thrust with a buttonhole stitch, at right angles to the bar, under the pinned loop and the other thread, which has just reappeared

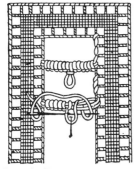 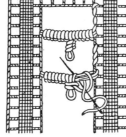

FIG. 8. BUTTONHOLE BAR WITH PINNED PICOT.　　FIG. 9. BUTTONHOLE BAR WITH PICOT.

from behind the foundation threads. This buttonhole stitch is then drawn tightly to the bar, and close to the last buttonhole stitch on the bar. The buttonholing is then continued until another picot is desired, when the process is repeated. When it is desired that more than one buttonhole stitch is to bind the picot in place, the first one is fastened sufficiently far from the bar to allow the others to be fitted closely between it and the bar, as is shown in Fig. 9.

Bar with Buttonhole Picot.

In making the buttonhole picot, the buttonholing of the prepared foundation threads is continued for six or more stitches beyond the point where the picot is to begin; or, in other words, the buttonholing is continued to the farther end of the proposed picot. The thread is then carried back to the sixth stitch, and passed between it and the seventh. It is then carried forward again and over the foundation threads close to the end of the buttonholing. Again it is carried back to the sixth buttonhole and secured. The needle is then thrust between the seventh and eighth buttonhole stitches. This is done to prevent the end of the picot from curling up out of place.

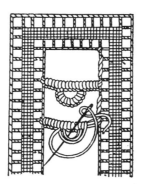

FIG. 10. BAR WITH BUTTON-HOLED PICOT.

The three foundation threads just made are then buttonholed until the picot is completed. The remainder of the bar is then buttonholed.

Bar with Two Rows of Dots.

One of the prettiest and most effective bar stitches consists of a foundation of two threads, upon which are worked two rows of buttonhole knots. One of these rows being on each side of the foundation threads, causes both sides of the finished bar to be exactly alike. The working thread is fastened to the braid at the right-hand end of the proposed bar, and is carried across to the opposite side, and there secured to the braid by passing the needle under one thread of the braid edge. It is then returned to the right side, and the buttonhole knots placed along the lower side or edge of the foundation threads.

The first stitch is a regular buttonhole stitch; the second is a reversed buttonhole stitch. This is worked in the following manner: The thread is held securely close to the just completed buttonhole stitch, by placing the left thumb upon it The loose end of the thread (the end on which the needle is threaded) is then drawn upwards toward the end of the thumb, and secured beneath it, thus forming a loop whose loose end is the one nearer the foundation threads. The needle is then passed back of the two foundation threads, over the upper or nearer thread of the thumb-held loop.

This reversed buttonhole stitch is drawn closely to the foundation threads. The result is two close buttonhole stitches secured by a tiny bar of the thread beneath them, and parallel to the foundation threads.

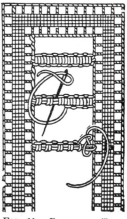

FIG. 11. BAR WITH TWO ROWS OF DOTS.

The next regular buttonhole stitch is placed upon the foundation threads just far enough from the former pair to permit the filling in of the space between by the pair of stitches to be worked from the other side. The reversed buttonhole stitch is then placed close to its companion, and the work so continued to the end of the foundation threads, which will show groups of two buttonhole stitches at regular intervals along its length.

The entire pattern is then reversed, bringing the unfinished side of the bar into position for completion. A group of the two buttonhole knots, the first regular and the second reversed, is then inserted in each of the spaces left for this purpose. The result is a closely covered bar of intricate appearance, and of a very braid-like effect. In fact, the ambitious worker may accomplish a piece of lace which, though containing a braid, is entirely hand made. To do this, a long, narrow strip of holland, or paper-lined cambric, is secured. The ends are then basted together, and a large hoop or ring thus formed. To this the two foundation threads are couched at regular intervals in a straight line, circling the hoop a number of times sufficient to furnish the required length of braid.

The pairs of buttonhole knots are then worked down the length of the threads on one side of the foundation threads. The holland hoop is then reversed, and the other side of the braid completed. The couching threads are then cut, and the dainty strip of "braid" released. The looplike appearance of the edges furnish very excellent openings for the needle, when the filling-in stitches are placed.

A wider braid may be secured by increasing the number of foundation threads, which may also be of a larger size than the filling-in stitches, if so desired. A very pretty network results from the use of this pair of regular and reversed buttonhole stitches. The work is done in rows, and is exactly like the Brussels net two-stitch, except that the second buttonhole stitch of each pair is reversed.

Raleigh Bars.

Another form of the buttonhole stitch bars is called the Raleigh bar. In this stitch the foundation bars are first laid throughout the space to be filled, using a coarse thread. These bars are often put in sufficiently loose that they may be twisted by the working thread several times before the next loop is made. This twisted length serves as another division, and increases the desired irregular appearance of the bars. After the foundation threads are all in place the buttonholing is accomplished with occasional picots, either pinned, lace, or bullion, worked at irregular intervals.

This stitch may be worked in a regular design of squares or triangles, but its chief beauty lies in its irregularity of form.

FIG. 12. RALEIGH BARS.

Bar with Picot Made in Bullion Stitch.

The foundation threads are prepared as for the plain buttonhole bar. These threads are covered with buttonhole stitches set close together until the place where the picot is to be placed is reached. The needle is then thrust part way through the

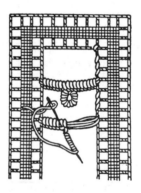

FIG. 13. BUTTONHOLED BAR WITH PICOT IN BULLION STITCH.

last buttonhole stitch, and the thread wound from left to right ten to twenty times around its point. These coils of thread must be drawn up closely and evenly along the length of the needle, but not so tightly that it is difficult or impossible to draw the needle through them. The left thumb is placed upon the coil, and the needle drawn through with the fingers of the right hand. The thread is pulled up so tightly that the coil is drawn almost into a semicircle. The buttonholing of the bar, against which the picot will rest securely, is continued until the point for the next picot is reached.

This coiling of the thread about the needle may be used in various ways. At the intersection of two twisted bars four bullion picots, meeting at the point of intersection, may be placed one between each right angle formed by the meeting of the twisted threads. See Fig. 14. A space filled with a network of lines at right angles, forming a checkerboard appearance when completed, with a quartet of these bullion picots at each intersection, is very effective. Closely worked networks may be embellished with good effect, as shown in Fig. 15. The needle in this case is passed down through the completed network at the point which is to be the centre of the figure,

FIG. 14. WAY OF WORKING QUATREFOIL IN BULLION STITCH.

and it reappears through the network at the point which is to be the outer end of the figure. The thread is then coiled around the point of the needle a sufficient number of times to fill the space between the disappearance and reappearance of the needle. The thumb is placed upon the coil, and the needle and thread drawn through until the coils are closely held together, but in a straight line. The needle is then thrust through the point where it made its former disappearance, and the coil lies on the network like a tiny leaf. Clusters of three or four of these coils meeting at a common centre are very effective.

The rounded bullion picot may also be worked upon a completed network, and when it is desired

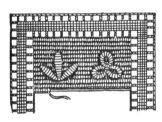

FIG. 15. TREFOILS IN BULLION STITCH WORKED ON BUTTONHOLED FOUNDATION.

to have it lie flat, a stitch may be taken through the network and the under-side of the picot, thus fastening the coiled loop securely to the network. Three bullion picot coils meeting at a centre, and with a worked stem attached, make a very pretty clover leaf. See Fig. 15.

Branched Bars, or Buttonholed Bars.

When it is desired to fill with bars spaces too wide to admit of the use of any of the bar stitches already given, branched bars will be very appropriate. They may be used with good effect, also, in filling in backgrounds. A piece of lace whose background is filled with branched buttonholed bars presents an especially rich appearance, and the extra time and labor necessary to accomplish this background is fully repaid by the beauty of the result.

The usual foundation of three threads is laid loosely across one corner of the space to be filled. These foundation threads are then closely buttonholed for about

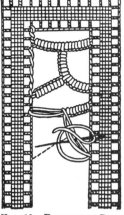

FIG. 16. BRANCHED BUT-TONHOLE BARS.

half their length, when the working thread is carried to the point selected for the end of the next loop. A second and third passing of the thread supplies the new foundation for this next loop, which is then buttonholed for half its length, when a third foundation is prepared.

This is continued until the spacing of the bars is accomplished. When in the placing of these bars it is necessary to complete the buttonholing of an unfinished bar before another is begun, it should be done, but the work should be so planned that the thread need never be broken, but will pass in a continuous circuit from bar to bar.

All the bars being placed, the work of completing the buttonholing of them is begun. The completion of one loop brings the working thread to the next unfinished bar awaiting completion, and so, one by one, the buttonholing of the bars is completed.

Bar with Lace Picot.

The lace picots are formed somewhat differently. See Fig. 17. The pin is placed as for the open pinned picots, and the thread passed around it and over and behind the foundation threads as

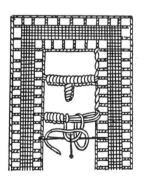

FIG. 17. BUTTONHOLE BAR WITH LACE PICOT.

before, but reappears *inside* or *between* the sides of the loop. The pin should be far enough from the bar to allow four buttonhole stitches to be set snugly upon the loop. The first one should be placed as near the pin as possible, in order to cover entirely the foundation loop. The other three stitches should follow the first ones closely and evenly, the last one lying against the last buttonhole stitch of the bar.

Point d'Anvers Bars.

For the filling in of leaf-shaped spaces, and used as an insertion for long narrow spaces, Point d'Anvers bars are equally good. The thread is fastened at the middle of one end of the space to be filled, and carried along the edge of the braid, one stitch to the right. It is then brought across the length of the space and attached to the braid, the same distance from the centre of the space as it is removed by the overcasting stitch at the opposite end. The thread is then carried by overcasting stitches a distance to the left, equally distant from the centre. It is then carried back in a parallel line to the opposite, or first end of the space, and fastened. The two lines of thread should

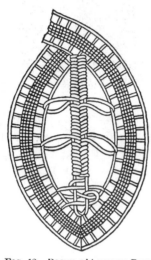

FIG. 18. POINT D'ANVERS BAR.

be perfectly parallel, and drawn tightly across the space, but not so tightly that they will draw the braid out of place. Keeping these foundation threads absolutely parallel, the working thread is passed in a darning or weaving stitch over and under them for the desired distance. Then the first pair of side loops or leaflets is made. The process of the weaving brings the working thread over the right bar. It is then passed behind it and over the left bar as during the preceding weaving, and is passed through the edge of the braid at the left side of the space, with the point of the needle toward the already woven end of the work. The thread is then passed under the left bar and over the right as before, and, with the point of the needle thrust from the woven end of the work, is carried through the edge of the braid, at the right side of the space. It is then brought under the right bar and under the last passing of the thread across the bars. It is then passed behind the left bar and over the right, and the two side loops being in place, the weaving of the bar is continued until the place for the next pair of side loops is reached, when the process is repeated. This is continued until the filling of the space is completed. For short connecting bars the Point d'Anvers bar is sometimes used without the side loops.

Wheels or Spiders.

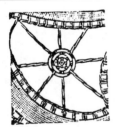

WHEELS or spiders are made on a foundation of plain twisted bars. The number of bars depends on the size of the space. They are cast across the space to be filled at distances from each other, and in such a manner that they all cross in the centre the space. They form diameters, whose halves of are radii of a circle. The first bar divides the space into halves and is overcast back to the starting-point. The thread is then overcast along the edge of the braid for the required distance and again carried across the space, crossing the first thread and entering the braid at the right place and overcast back to its beginning. This is repeated until the last bar has been overcast to the centre, when all the threads may be fastened together with a buttonhole knot or not, as preferred. The spider is then woven.

This is accomplished by passing the needle over and under the different radii formed by the bars and keeping the woven thread drawn tightly or snugly to the centre. This is continued until the spider is of sufficient size, when the remaining radius or half bar is overcast and the thread cut.

There are various kinds of spiders. The simplest is shown in Fig. 19, and is formed by the regular over and under weaving of the radii, and results in keeping every alternate radius on the

FIG. 19. SPINNING WHEEL. FIG. 20. SPINNING WHEEL.

upper side of the spider when finished. The thread occasionally passed between the two twisted threads of a radius will keep the circling thread of the spider from rolling upon itself. Another effect is produced by skipping one radius in every circuit of the thread forming the spider. This alternates the thread

FIG. 21. SPINNING WHEEL WITH KNOTTED CIRCLES.

over and under the same radius and hides them all from view, as shown in Fig. 20.

In many uneven places the putting in of the bars may be so regulated that their completion permits a final half bar, or a radius, instead of a diameter. This is carried to the centre and the spider woven as before. Here the odd number of radii admits, in fact necessitates, the continual alternating of the bars or radii.

A pretty result is obtained by circling the spider with one, two, or more rows of the thread, tied at each radius with a buttonhole knot as shown in Fig. 21. These circles are to be perfectly true and equally distant from the spider. To form these circles the last radius is overcast two or three times, and the series of knots tied around the spider at each radius. Upon completing the circle a few more overcasting stitches carries the thread a sufficient distance, and a second circle is knotted in. When enough circles have been made, the rest of the radius is overcast and the thread fastened off. Smaller spiders, Point de Venise "shells," and other similar stitches may be placed at the tying of each knot, and become very effective.

Spinning Wheel Rosettes.

The spinning wheel rosettes, Figs. 22 and 23, also called ribbed wheels, are made on a founda-

tion of twisted threads crossing in the centre similar to the foundation threads for the spider or wheel before given. The working thread is carried under two radii, drawn up closely and firmly in place. The needle is then passed under the second of these radii, and also under the next one (see

FIG. 22. SPINNING WHEEL ROSETTE.

Fig. 23), and the thread is again drawn into position. In this manner the working thread is always carried back over the last radius under which it passed, and forward under the next one. This results in a raised twist or coil over each radius as shown in the finished wheel, Fig. 22. When the lace is being made with the right side next the pattern, these ribbed wheels must be made wrong side up. To do this the needle is thrust under one radius at a time, with the point of the needle toward both the worker and the last radius around which the thread has passed. The thread is then carried over the radius and on to the next one, where the process is repeated. The two ways may be combined, and the result is a very effective rosette that

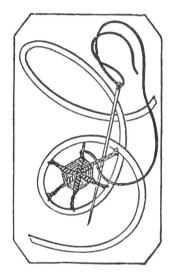

FIG. 23. DETAIL OF SPINNING WHEEL ROSETTE.

is often seen in drawn work. The centre is worked with the coil on the upper or working side for a sufficient space, when for a similar space the work is reversed, and the coil worked on the under side.

Insertions.

Plain Russian Stitch.

THE plain Russian stitch, Fig. 24, is the simplest of the insertions, and, like all insertions, is suitable for long, narrow spaces in the design of the pattern. This is accomplished by a series of buttonhole stitches, alternating from one side of the space to the other.

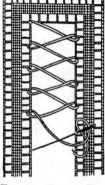

FIG. 24. PLAIN RUSSIAN STITCH.

The thread is securely fastened in the upper, or farther, left-hand corner. It is then brought forward over the space and held against the pattern by the left thumb. The needle is then thrust through the braid on the right side of the space, with the needle pointing directly across toward the braid at the left side. The thread is carried through the braid and again secured by the left thumb. The work is then repeated from the left side of the space, with the needle pointing toward the right side. Holding the thread down with the thumb makes it impossible to make a wrong twist, as the needle never passes under the thread held in this way.

This stitch may be varied by tying each crossing thread in the middle with a buttonhole knot.

Twisted Russian Stitch.

The twisted Russian stitch, Fig. 25, is a trifle more complicated. As in the former, the stitches alternate from right to left, but the method of holding the thread down with the left thumb differs.

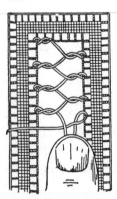

FIG. 25. TWISTED RUSSIAN STITCH.

The thread is fastened at the upper left-hand corner and carried forward over the space to be filled. The thumb is then placed upon it as near the point of fastening as is practical, and the thread is brought to the right and again slipped under the thumb, forming an open loop, upon both sides of which the thumb rests. The needle is then thrust through the edge of the braid at the right, with the point directed to the opposite left. It is then passed over the right-hand thread of the loop, under the left-hand thread, and drawn up. It is well to leave the thumb on the loop till the stitch is nearly completed, as it avoids tangling the thread and causes a more even twist.

Again the thumb holds down the thread, which is then brought up on the left side and slipped under the thumb as before. The needle is thrust through the braid at the left over the loose side of the loop and under the other or right side. This is repeated until the space is filled.

The same effect may be produced by using the plain Russian stitch, and with an overcasting stitch producing the extra twist; but this takes more time and is not as even in results.

Column Stitch.

Column stitch, shown in Fig. 26, is a combination of plain and twisted Russian stitch. Each stitch on one side of the space to be filled is a plain Russian stitch, while all those on the other side are twisted Russian stitches, with the working thread passed three or more times around the already twisted thread. This stitch makes a very

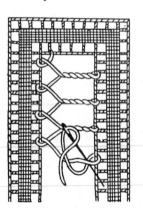

FIG. 26. COLUMN STITCH.

pretty insertion for either straight or curved spaces. In the latter, the twisted side of the stitch may be at the outer curve of the place to be filled, and the twisted threads will radiate evenly outwards. The opposite effect may be obtained by reversing the order of the stitches, when the coils of the twisted side will converge, and, if the curve is pronounced, will almost meet, and have the appearance of the spokes of a wheel.

Insertion of Single Buttonhole Stitch.

Along both sides of the long, narrow space to be filled, a row of Brussels net (single buttonhole) stitches is worked very evenly and quite loosely. If the space is a curve the stitches along the inner or smaller side of the space must be made closer together, in order that the stitches of the two rows will be in pairs, with each loop of the inner side between two loops of the opposite side. This

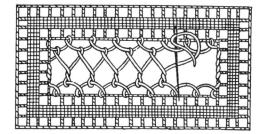

FIG. 27. INSERTION OF SINGLE BUTTONHOLE STITCH.

arrangement places a loop opposite every buttonhole stitch on either side of the space, and makes an even, regular spacing for the Russian stitch, which connects the two rows of net stitches. To do this the thread is fastened at one end of one of the rows of net stitches, and is carried from side to side, looping into each net stitch in turn. This connecting stitch may be either plain or twisted Russian stitch, or, as shown in the cut, may be plain Russian on one side, and twisted Russian on the other. Column stitch may also be used.

Insertion of Buttonhole Stitch.

A very pleasing variation of the foregoing stitch is made by arranging the single rows of Brussels net stitches with the loops directly opposite each other. The space between the two rows is then filled with a row of double Russian stitch. This is made by placing two stitches of either plain or

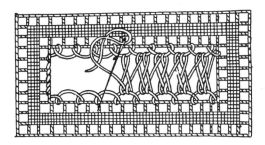

FIG. 28. INSERTION OF BUTTONHOLE STITCH.

twisted Russian stitch in each loop. Where a close or compact insertion is desired, triple or quadruple Russian stitch may be used. This is accomplished by placing three or four Russian stitches in each loop. For all ordinary purposes double, or at most triple, Russian stitch is all that is necessary. A more or less compact effect will be gained by using a finer or coarser thread.

Insertion with Cones.

When a heavy, showy effect is desired, cone insertion may be used. The working thread is fastened to the middle of one end of the space to be filled. A single row of plain Russian stitch is worked throughout the length of the space. The stitches of this Russian insertion must be placed at regular intervals, but somewhat far apart. Upon this as a foundation, the cones are placed. These cones are worked over each pair of threads diverging from the braid. The working thread is attached to the point of divergence of the first two threads, which is, in other words, the point where the thread forming the Russian stitch is first attached to the braid. The thread is then carried by means of the needle over and under these two diverging threads until a closely woven, cone-shaped figure, reaching from its point at the edge of the

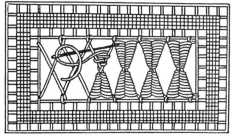

FIG. 29. INSERTION WITH CONES.

braid to the middle of the width of the space, is finished.

The working thread is then carried by means of a series of overcasting or twisting threads along the other half of the thread which is to form one foundation or side of the first cone on the other side of the space. The braid being reached, the thread is carried through the open margin of the braid at the point where the thread of the Russian stitch enters. A cone is woven over these threads, and the working thread carried as before to the adjoining threads on the opposite side of the space.

Insertion with Reversed Cones.

A still more massive effect is produced by reversing the cones, and in this way having their bases rest upon the braid along the sides of the space to be filled, and the points of each pair of opposite cones meeting at the centre of the width of the space.

The first row of plain Russian stitch is worked throughout the length of the space as before. A second row of the same stitch is then worked over the first in such a manner that the working thread is attached to the braid just half way between the attachments of the first row. This results in the threads of the two rows crossing

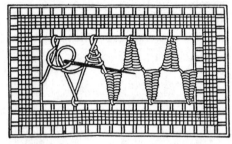

FIG. 30. INSERTION WITH REVERSED CONES.

each other exactly in the centre of the width of the space. The working thread is then carried over and under the first two threads that will meet in the centre. The weaving thread having arrived at the point where the threads cross each other, the point or apex of the opposite cone is reached, and the weaving continued over these two threads until the second cone is completed at the arrival of the working thread at the edge of the opposite braid. The succeeding pairs of cones are worked in the same manner.

Beaded Insertion or D'Alencon.

As in Fig. 27 a row of Brussels net stitches, with the long loops opposite each other, is worked on both sides of the narrow space to be filled. The working thread is then carried once around the end loop to which it is nearest, and that loop and the one opposite are then joined together by four connecting loops, which must lie in close parallel lines. They must never cross or lie upon each other. To make these loops the needle is thrust under the loop at the right side

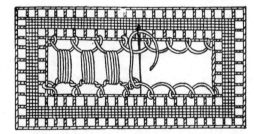

FIG. 31. BEADED INSERTION, OR D'ALENCON BARS.

of the space, across to the opposite loop, under which also the needle passes, and is drawn out between the loop and the braid. This is repeated

the other three times necessary to make the "bead" of four threads. At the completion of one "bead," the working thread is carried once around the filled net loop, and once around the next one, which is then joined, as was the first pair, to the next opposite net loop. This brings all the overcasting of the net loops, when carrying the thread from one pair of stitches to the next, on the same side of the work.

Insertion with Small Wheels.

To make this pretty stitch, the space to be filled is first covered with an insertion of plain Russian stitch, having the distance between the stitches on either side of the braid just twice as far apart as you desire them to be in the completed work. A second row of plain Russian stitch is then worked over the first, with the stitches on either side of the braid exactly half

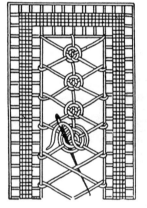

FIG. 32. INSERTION WITH SMALL WHEELS.

way between those of the former row. The threads of the two rows of stitches cross each other in the middle of the space, and form a series of diamonds and triangles, and the result is a very pretty insertion without further work.

To place the wheels at the points of intersection of the threads, the working thread is first carried to the middle of one end of the space, and then to the crossing of the first two threads. Here, if desired, a knot may fasten them together, but it is not necessary, and the effect is better if the weaving of the wheels is begun over the crossing of the loose threads. There being an uneven number of threads (five), the weaving thread will alternate over and under into a basket weave that will hold the work securely in place. The completion of each wheel must be on the side nearest the next wheel to be worked. The needle is passed behind or under two threads of the finished wheel, and to the next point of intersection (see Fig. 32), where the next wheel is worked.

When it is desired to make the work more elaborate, half wheels may be worked at each or at every alternate connection of the thread with the braid. These half wheels are formed by weaving

16

the working thread through the edge of the braid, over and under the two diverging threads, and through the edge of the braid on the other side until the half wheel is of sufficient size.

Bars of Point d'Angleterre.

Insertion with big wheels. When a more showy insertion is desired, a design with larger wheels may be used. To accomplish this a thread is carried lengthwise across the middle of the space to be filled and fastened into position in the braid at the ends of the space. The working thread is then carried by means of overcasting stitches along the open edge of the braid to the corner of the space. A loose loop is then formed across this end of the space by passing the working thread through the opposite corner, and leaving the loop loose enough to form the vertical half of a diamond-shaped space. The thread is then carried by means of overcasting stitches a sufficient distance along the braid at the side of the space to be filled.

The needle is then thrust over the former loop, under the horizontal thread that was first carried across the length of the space, and again over the thread of the loop. It is then carried to the opposite side of the space and fastened to the edge of the braid at exactly the same distance from the corner as is its opposite end from the other corner. The thread is then carried directly across the space from one end of this second or inverted, loop to the other, and just tightly enough to form a straight line across the space. This thread is then overcast to the middle of the space, where a wheel of four or more circlings of the threads is woven with the thread passing each time over the same threads of the intersection.

Should the circles of the resulting wheels be prone to slip out of place the needle may be thrust between the two threads of the twisted length, but with careful work this will not be necessary. The wheel being completed, the thread is carried back of it to its opposite side, where the other half of the straight thread is overcast and the needle

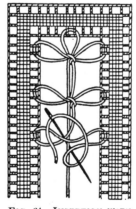

passed through the braid. From this point a new loop is formed, reaching from one end of the straight twisted thread to the other. The thread is then carried along the braid and the work continued.

The beauty of this insertion lies in the exactness with which it is made. The space between the straight threads must always be exactly the same. and the loops must all be of the same length, so that each diamond may be exactly like its neighbors, and surround a wheel exactly the size of all the other wheels.

Insertion with Branches.

These are two very pretty leaf or branched insertions. They are especially appropriate for oval or leaf-shaped openings. The working thread is fastened to the middle of one end of the space to be filled and carried to the middle of the opposite end of the space, where it is carried by the needle under four or five threads of the open edge of the braid. This ensures the rounded open shape of the leaflet. The needle is then thrust, in a similar manner, under the same number of threads, along the left side of the braid near the upper end of the space, with the needle pointed upwards. The loop so formed is left slack or loose enough to form the loose, open loops at the braid edges, and, for the middle of the loop, to lie close to the lengthwise thread or midrib to which it is soon to be tied.

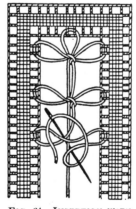

FIG. 33. INSERTION WITH LARGE WHEELS.

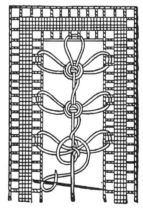

FIG. 34. INSERTION WITH BRANCHES.   FIG. 35 INSERTION WITH BRANCHES.

The thread is then carried horizontally across the space, and the needle thrust with its point directed downwards under four or five threads of the braid. The thread is then carried in the midrib, and the needle thrust behind or under the first or left-side leaflet, the midrib and the second or right-side leaflet, and under the point of the needle, which is then drawn through, and the thread tightened in the buttonhole knot which results. This completes the first group of leaflets. The needle is then again thrust into the braid at the left side of the space, and the second pair of leaflets begun.

After the leaflets are tied together with the buttonhole knot, the working thread may be carried alternately over the leaves and under the midrib, circling the knot a sufficient number of times to make a wheel or rosette at the intersection of the leaflets.

Leaf Insertion.

An insertion with leaves in darning stitch is excellent where a heavy, rich effect is desired. The working thread is attached to the end of the space at which the first terminal leaf of the insertion is to be worked. This thread is then carried to the opposite end of the space, thrust through a single loop of the braid, and carried back, untwisted, to the starting point. It is then carried to the left side of the space, and attached to the braid at that point by having the needle thrust under not more than two threads of the open edge of the braid. The thread is then carried to the right side of the space, and caught into the braid in the same manner at a point exactly opposite the point of attachment on the left side. The thread is then brought back to the midrib, or two long threads. The needle is then thrust behind all the threads, and drawn up in a tight buttonhole knot, as is shown in the illustration for insertion with branches, Fig. 34.

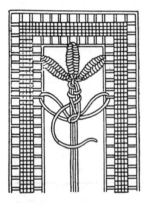

FIG. 36. LEAF INSERTION.

The thread is then carried, for a second time, around the terminal or first leaf, which is then filled from point to knot with a close succession of darning stitches over and under the threads outlining the leaf. At the completion of this leaf, the thread is carried around the left leaf, and passed again through the braid at its point. This makes three foundation threads on one side, and two on the other side of the leaf. When an effect not so heavy is desired, the thread passing all around the leaf may be omitted. This makes two foundation threads on one side and one on the other, and is somewhat more difficult to darn. This leaf is then darned, after which the leaf on the right side is finished in a similar manner.

The outlines for the second pair of side leaves are then made and tied to the midrib with a buttonhole knot as were the first two. The working thread is then passed one and a half times around the two threads of the midrib that is to form the middle of the next trio of leaves. The needle is passed through the knot each time at the point of this leaf. This is at the base of the completed trio of leaves above. The middle leaf is then filled with the darning stitch, as are each of the side leaves. The work proceeds in this way until the entire space is filled.

Cluster Insertion.

This is one of the most charming and useful of the insertions, and the ease with which it is made increases its popularity. It is equally appropriate for straight or curved spaces. Two twisted parallel bars are worked, and the thread for the third bar carried across and overcast nearly to the middle, when the three bars, two twisted and one incomplete, are joined by fine, tight buttonhole stitches, worked over them close together. The twisting of the third bar is then completed.

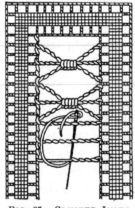

FIG. 37. CLUSTER INSERTION.

The first and third bars of each group should be just loose or slack enough to admit of their being fastened, by the buttonhole stitches, to the middle bar, without drawing the braid out of place. The first bar of each succeeding trio should be placed close to the last bar of the preceding group.

Network Stitches.

Single Net Stitch.

SINGLE net stitch, called Brussels point (Point de Bruxelles), is the foundation of many of the net stitches, and consists of rows of buttonhole stitches worked loosely. The beauty of this stitch lies in the evenness and regularity of the stitches. The loops should all be of the same length, and the buttonhole stitches must fall in even lines, forming parallel diagonal lines both from the upper right-hand corner toward the lower left, and from the upper left toward the lower right. The chief difficulty in working this stitch is at the ends of the rows. The loops form diamond-shaped spaces, and great care must be taken at the ends of each row to so place the stitches that the fractional spaces shall be true parts of whole spaces. A little care in regulating the distance along its edge, in carrying the thread to position for the next row of stitches, and trial placing of the thread

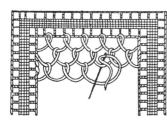

FIG. 38. SINGLE NET STITCH.

to note the effect, will soon lead to great proficiency in this respect. Every loop should, in the following row, receive a buttonhole stitch, and all widening and narrowing must be done at the ends of the rows. The stitches must be kept even, and the loops of the same size. When this is done, the widening and narrowing attends to itself. The worker should never attempt to retain the same number of stitches in every row throughout an irregular space. The space must regulate the number of stitches, and accommodate only just so many as there is room for when keeping them at their regular size. This stitch may be made with large open loops, giving a very open, lacy effect, or the loops may be made small, and consequently the work much more close in appearance. Both for background and for filling in, this is a very useful stitch, and will be found especially desirable for large spaces.

Venice originated Point proper, which may have been worked there in isolated instances before 1600, but it came prominently forward towards the middle of the seventeenth century. Designs given in the pattern books of the sixteenth century are all of the Reticella type, and cannot be bought under designation of real Point.

Double Net Stitch.

Double net stitch, also called Point de Sorrento, shown in Fig. 39, and the two stitch, is made in the same manner as is the single net stitch, except that here the loops between the buttonhole stitches are somewhat less rounded; that is, they are drawn a little more closely, and, instead of one buttonhole stitch, two are made

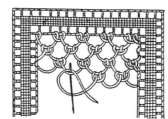

FIG 39. DOUBLE NET STITCH.

close together. In order to keep them thus near each other, the second stitch must be drawn tightly up to the first. The same rules as to evenness, regularity, widening, and narrowing that are given for the single net stitch apply to this as well as all other net stitches. The two stitch, while taking twice as long as the single net stitch, is more easily made perfect, as the two stitches aid in keeping the work firm and true. This is one of the most satisfactory of the net stitches.

Three Stitch.

The three stitch is also called Point de Sorrento, and is identical with the two stitch, except that three close buttonhole stitches are used instead of two. This results in a heavier, more solid effect. If a still closer effect is desired, four buttonhole stitches may be used. In this case the intervening loop should be just long enough to accommodate the four stitches that are to be placed in it when working the next row. These stitches may be combined and varied in different ways. A good effect is produced by alternating first a row of

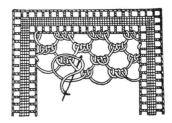

FIG. 40. THREE STITCH.

single net stitch, and then a row of three stitch. Three rows of single net stitch may be followed by three rows of the two stitch. In fact it is the variation and combination of these stitches that form many of the intricate lace stitches.

Buttonholed Net Stitch.

Where a network showing a heavy effect is desired, buttonholed net stitch is excellent. A row of Brussels net is worked with wide, regular loops. Into each of these loops is worked a regular number of buttonhole stitches sufficient to completely fill the loop from one buttonhole stitch to the next. The third row is like the first — a row of wide Brussels net stitches. Each stitch is placed in the little loop between the groups of buttonhole stitches of the second row. The fourth row is like the second. When finished the groups of close buttonhole stitches should form vertical rows across the space filled. Care should be taken not to draw the work to one

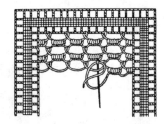

FIG. 41. BUTTONHOLED NET STITCH.

side or the other, and in this way pull these rows out of the vertical. In an oblong or long pointed space, the group of close stitches at the middle of the top row should extend to the extreme point of the opposite end. As buttonhole stitch is made more readily from the left to the right, the rows of close stitches may be worked in that direction, and the open rows from right to left. This is accomplished by beginning the work at the upper right-hand corner.

Another buttonholed net stitch is shown in Fig. 42. The first row of this stitch is formed by working three buttonhole stitches rather close together (with just a little more than room between them for another stitch), and then beginning a second group of three stitches sufficiently far from the first to make the long loop between the two groups equal in length to the space occupied by the groups of three stitches. In the second row the long loops are nearly filled with a close row of buttonhole stitches,

FIG. 42. BUTTONHOLED NET STITCH.

and a single buttonhole stitch is placed in each of the two loops formed between the groups of three stitches of the previous row. The third row is like the first, and the fourth row is like the second. The result is a more open, fanciful arrangement of stitches than the preceding pattern, but, like it, the rows of close buttonhole stitches form vertical lines from end to end of the space filled.

Point de Venise Stitches.

Point de Venise, often called shell, seed, or side stitch, is very popular, and suitable either for edgings or for the filling in of spaces. For the former a single row of "shells" is worked around the edge of the completed lace. For filling in spaces, the work is done in rows. Beginning at the right-hand corner of the space to be filled, a row of even, rather loose buttonhole stitches is worked. The thread is carried down the side of the braid the distance equal to the width of a stitch. Into the first loop is placed a buttonhole stitch, and as in the Petit Point de Venise, this stitch is tied by another buttonhole stitch worked sideways. This stitch should be far enough from the top of the buttonhole stitch being covered to accommodate three other rather tightly drawn buttonhole stitches, which are worked side by side and each above its predecessor until the last one covers the end of the loop upon which the shell is built. This shell being finished, a buttonhole stitch is placed in the next loop of the first row, and another shell worked upon it. In placing the stitches of the shell, the needle is thrust under and at right angles with both threads of the buttonhole stitch to be covered.

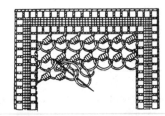

FIG. 43. POINT DE VENISE.

The size of the shell depends upon the number of side stitches worked, and upon how tightly they are drawn. Four stitches is the usual number. A more curved effect is obtained if the first stitch is quite tightly drawn, and the others made looser. The row of shells being completed, the third row is worked. This consists of a row of single net stitches, one buttonhole stitch being placed between each shell, and the loop drawn up so as to fit like a saucer around the shell above it. This gives a rather close effect, and is decidedly pretty. Where a more open result is desired, the loops may be made larger. In this case the loops upon which the shells are made must also be made larger, as all the loops throughout must be of the same size.

In widening, very great care must be taken not to make the loops larger, or stint the number of shells, and so give the latter part of the work a straggly, loose appearance, very different from the first part.

Another variation of Point de Venise is

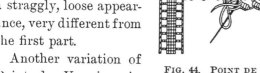

FIG. 44. POINT DE VENISE.

shown in Fig. 44. In this the row of single net stitches is omitted, and a shell is worked upon every loop of each row. This causes the shells of the first and third rows to slant toward the left while the shells of the second and fourth rows slant toward the right. Worked in this way, the result is a heavy, sumptuous stitch, and is very beautiful. Perhaps the fact that it is so much more slowly worked is the reason we find it less often in use than the more favored variety with the row of net stitches.

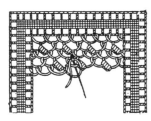

FIG. 45. POINT DE VENISE.

Still another Point de Venise stitch, Fig. 45, is varied as well as made more open, and worked in less time by omitting every other shell. The alternating rows of Brussels net stitches are made as in Fig. 43. In the second row a loop is made, and a shell worked upon it. A second loop has the shell omitted. On the third loop a shell is worked. Alternating in this way the row is finished. Great care must be used in putting in the net stitches of the third row to avoid skipping a stitch. A stitch must be placed close upon each side of every shell of the row above. This ensures a buttonhole stitch upon each side of the single stitches between the shells. When finished the pattern shows rows of parallel diagonal lines of shells across the space filled. The beauty of this stitch depends upon its perfect regularity.

A pleasing arrangement of Point de Venise stitches is made by working one net stitch beneath which three or four side stitches are placed. This stitch may be worked in two ways. The loops between the single net stitches are made sufficiently loose to admit of the placing of the three or four side stitches, which fill the loop until it is almost straight. The work is begun at the upper left

corner, and when the opposite upper right corner is reached the thread is fastened to the braid and carried down its edge for a space equal to the width of the stitches of the

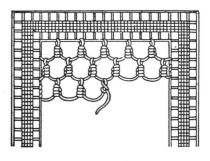

FIG. 46. POINT DE VENISE.

first row. The second row is like the first, except that it proceeds from right to left. This method causes the side stitches of every alternate row to point to the left, and the intervening rows to point to the right. When it is desired to have all the side stitches lie in the same direction, the thread, at the completion of the first row, is carried to the left side by thrusting the needle once through each loop of the first row, and in this way carrying it across the space. This gives a corded effect to the loops. The thread is carried down the side of the braid, and the working of the second row is begun.

These Point de Venise stitches may be distinguished from each other by calling them according to the number of stitches used. The two-one Point de Venise stitch consists of two net stitches and one side stitch. The two-two stitch is composed of two net stitches and two side stitches. The three-one is made of three net stitches and one side stitch, while one net stitch and three side stitches is called the one-three Point de Venise.

Petit Point de Venise.

This stitch may be worked openly or as compactly as desired. The first method gives an open lacy effect, while the second shows a stitch almost solid in appearance, so little space is there between the stitches. Beginning at the upper left corner, a loose buttonhole stitch is first made, and a second buttonhole stitch is worked sideways over or around the first one. This is drawn tightly, and so secures the first stitch

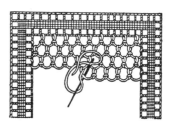

FIG. 47. PETIT POINT DE VENISE.

in place. A second loose buttonhole stitch is

21

worked and tied by a "side" stitch, and this is continued to the end of the row. The thread is then carried down the braid for a distance equal to the width of the stitch. The second row is then worked in the same way as the first. This is continued until the space is finished.

A pretty Point de Venise stitch is formed by a union of the double net stitch, or Point de Sorrento, and the side stitch. The thread is fastened at the upper left corner of the space to be filled,

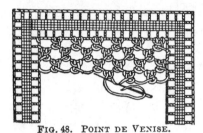

FIG. 48. POINT DE VENISE.

and two net stitches set close together along the edge of the upper braid. These are bound together by a third buttonhole stitch set sideways across the base of the two net stitches. To accomplish this, after the second net stitch is in place,

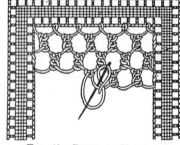

FIG. 49. POINT DE VENISE.

the needle is thrust in the loop at the left of the two stitches, and drawn up closely in the buttonhole knot. Two more net stitches are then made in the edge of the braid at a distance from the first pair equal to the space they occupy, and with

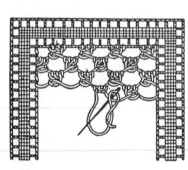

FIG. 50. POINT DE VENISE.

the connecting loop drawn sufficiently tight to make the rows of stitches lie in straight, parallel lines. The side stitch is then placed in position beneath them, and the work continued to the end of the row. The second row is like the first, except that in working from right to left the direction of the stitches is reversed.

Variations of this stitch are formed by placing two side stitches beneath to guard the two net stitches, or by working three net stitches with one side stitch. Other variations of these useful stitches will suggest themselves to the lace maker.

Point d'Espagne — Spanish Point Stitches.

The Spanish point stitches form a group of very distinctive difference from the other lace stitches. Instead of the scalloped or looped appearance of the foregoing stitches, they produce a rectangular effect of horizontal parallel lines connected at right angles by the vertical twisted stitches. Their appearance is very open and effective, and, besides making very good filling-in stitches for the design of the pattern, they give excellent results when used to fill in backgrounds. As in all the filling stitches, the lines must be perfectly even and regular to obtain a satisfactory effect.

Open Spanish Point.

The long effect of the stitch is the result of the extra twist given the thread by the method of forming the stitch. The thread is fastened at the upper left corner of the space and carried down the edge of the left-hand braid for the required distance, or the width of the stitch, which varies in length according to the degree of fineness or coarseness of the working thread. The thumb of the left hand is placed upon the thread as near the braid as is conveniently practical. The thread is then carried to

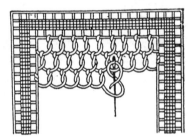

FIG. 51. OPEN SPANISH POINT.

the right of the thumb, and again placed under it in such a way that the thumb holds down both sides of the loop which is beneath it. The needle is then thrust at the proper place through the upper braid, over the nearer thread of the loop, and under the farther thread. The thumb is kept on the loop until the working thread has been drawn nearly to the completion of the stitch. This is repeated to the end of the row, when the work is reversed and the second row of stitches put in. This is accomplished by forming the loop on the left side of the thumb, proceeding as before. This method of working the stitch is clearly illustrated in Fig. 51.

Spanish Point.

The first row of this stitch is worked just as is the first row of the preceding one. At the completion of the row the working thread is car-

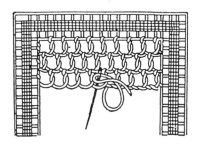

FIG. 52. SPANISH POINT.

ried back to the left side of the space by passing the needle once through each loop of the first row and drawing the thread up tight. Only one stitch can successfully be taken up by the needle at a time, as putting the needle through several loops and then drawing the thread is very apt to pull the stitches out of place, and so make them slant instead of maintaining the desired vertical position.

When the working thread has reached the left side of the space, it is carried down the edge of the braid and the second row of loop stitches worked.

Spanish Point.

A very pretty variation of this stitch is formed by placing the stitches in groups. See Fig. 53.

Three Spanish point stitches are worked at regular, somewhat close intervals, as in the former stitch. Space enough for two stitches is omitted, and the first stitch of the next group of three stitches is placed just where the sixth stitch would have been worked had not the stitches belonging to the fourth and fifth spaces been omitted.

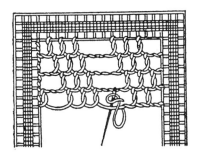

FIG. 53. SPANISH POINT.

These groups of three stitches are continued across the space and the working thread entered into the braid. The needle is then thrust once through each of the two smaller loops and twice through the longer loop that separates the groups of stitches. When the thread has been brought clear across the space, it is entered into the braid and carried by overcasting stitches the necessary distance along the edge of the braid.

The second row of the groups of stitches is then begun. The first stitch of the first group is placed in the loop between the first and second stitches of the row above. The second stitch is placed in the other or following loop, and the third or last stitch of the group is placed on the long loop just beyond the third stitch of the row above. This is continued across the space. The thread is carried back to the left side of the space as before by thrusting it through the loops of the last row.

Each succeeding row is begun by placing the first stitch to the right of the first stitch of the preceding row, and the result is a series of diagonal lines of stitches in groups of three, extending from the upper left corner of the space toward the lower right corner.

Another combination consists of a group of six Spanish point stitches set close together, followed by a space wide enough for four stitches. See Fig. 54. Another group of six stitches is worked and followed by another space the size of the

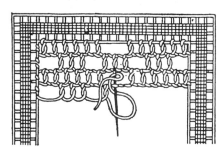

FIG. 54. SPANISH POINT.

former one. This is continued until the braid at the opposite side is reached. The thread is then carried in the regular way back to the left side of the space. A stitch is worked in the loop following the second stitch of the first group of six stitches of the row above. This is followed by a stitch in each of the two following loops, and results in a trio of stitches directly under the middle of the group of six stitches above.

Three other stitches are worked in the open space or long loop, and these are followed by another trio of stitches worked under the middle of the second group of six stitches above. This is continued to the end of the space. The third row is like the first and the fourth is like the second.

Another arrangement of the Spanish stitches is shown in Fig. 55. The first row consists of stitches placed closely together at regular intervals across the space. At the completion of each row the working thread is overcast back to the left side of the space. The second row consists of four stitches placed in each of the first four loops between the stitches of the preceding row. One loop is omitted and another group of four stitches worked. This is continued across the space. The third row consists of groups of three stitches placed in the loops between the groups of four stitches of the second row. The fourth row consists of groups of two stitches placed between the groups of three of the preceding row, and the fifth row consists of one stitch between the two of the fourth row and forms the point of the triangle. The sixth row is a repetition of the first, and a row of new points is begun. A long, narrow diamond design may be made by reversing the order of the stitches at the beginning of the second row of points. To accomplish this a row of two stitches would be worked on the row following the fifth row of single stitches. This would be increased to three stitches in the next row, and so continued until the ninth row would be reached and worked like the first.

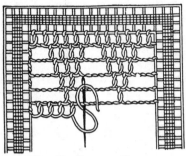

FIG. 55. SPANISH POINT.

Spanish Point Insertion.

Long, narrow spaces may be filled with Spanish point stitches. Row after row of these stitches are worked along the length of the space, and may be so continued until the opposite edge of the space is reached, when the returning thread is used to attach the last row of stitches to the adjoining braid. In the case of spaces of irregular width, when only one row of stitches remains to be worked at the narrow parts of the space, the pattern is turned around, and the last row worked from the edge of the second braid, and each stitch, as the work proceeds, is attached by overcasting stitches to the already finished rows. Where the space is wider, longer stitches are formed by increasing the number of the twistings of the working thread around the stitch, as shown in the illustration. A little practice will enable the worker to adapt this stitch to spaces of different shapes.

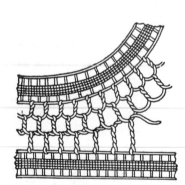

FIG. 56. SPANISH POINT INSERTION.

Shell Insertion.

One of the most beautiful of all the insertions is composed of Spanish point stitches. The thread is fastened at the upper left corner of the space, or, in the case of an oval-shaped space, in the upper point. It is then carried by overcasting stitches down the left edge of the braid, a distance equal to the length of the Spanish point stitches. Into the middle of the braid, at the end of the space, four Spanish point stitches are worked, entering the same point in the braid. The thread is then attached to the edge of the braid at the right side of the space exactly the same distance from the corner as it is on the left side. The working thread is overcast once (or twice if the space be. wide) over the straight thread connected with the braid at the right side and once over each small loop between the Spanish point stitches, and, finally, once or twice over the thread connected with the braid at the left side.

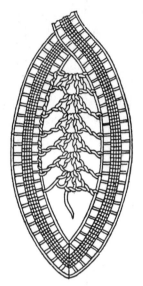

FIG. 57. SHELL INSERTION.

It is then carried down the side of the braid the same distance as before, and four Spanish point stitches are placed between the second and third stitches of the first row. The thread is again fastened to the braid and overcast through the stitches to the left side of the space, and the work so continued until the space is filled.

Spanish Net Stitches.

The various arrangements and groupings of the Spanish net stitches form many beautiful and practical networks. Where a very close effect is desired, good results may be obtained by working row after row of close Spanish net stitches as shown in Fig. 58. Beginning at the upper left corner of the space, a row of Spanish net stitches is worked, with just space

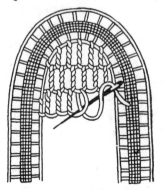

FIG. 58. SPANISH NET.

enough between them to provide room for the stitches of the next row, one of which is placed on each tiny loop between the stitches of the preceding row. The second row may be worked from right to left, or, when a heavier effect is desired, the working thread may be carried to the left side by overcasting it once through each loop.

Double Spanish Net

Is the more open result obtained when the stitches are arranged in pairs. Two close Spanish net stitches are worked; a space sufficient to accommodate two more stitches is left open, and is followed by a second pair of stitches similar to the first pair. In other words, the stitches are exactly as in close Spanish net, except that every other pair of stitches is omitted. In this stitch, to obtain good results, it is necessary on reaching the end of each row to overcast the working thread through the loops back to the left side of the space. This maintains the parallel effect desired. The second row is exactly like the first, except that the pairs of stitches are placed upon the long bar between the pairs of stitches of the preceding row.

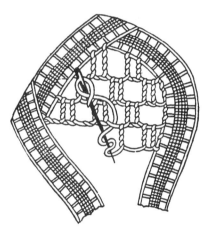

FIG. 59. DOUBLE SPANISH NET.

Triple Spanish Net.

Still another arrangement is called triple Spanish net, or treble Point d'Espagne. This arrangement is exactly like the double Spanish net, except that the stitches are in groups of threes instead of being in pairs as in the double Spanish stitch.

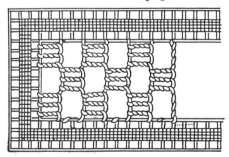

FIG. 60. TRIPLE SPANISH NET.

Grouped Spanish Net.

This illustration shows an arrangement of Spanish net stitches in groups of six. Six close Spanish net stitches are worked from left to right across the space, with exactly the same space between the groups as they themselves occupy, so that the groups of six stitches of the next row, which will be worked on the bars between the spaces of the first row, will exactly fill them, with no room to spare, and no crowding. Great care must be taken to keep the long loops or bars between the groups drawn sufficiently tight to keep the lower edge of the stitches exactly parallel with the upper edge all along the length of the row.

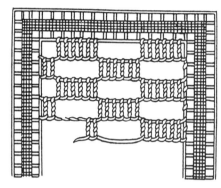

FIG. 61. SPANISH NET.

When the first row is completed the thread is carried to the left side of the space by overcasting it once through each little loop between the stitches of each group, and several times, carefully and smoothly, over the long loop or bar between the groups. The second row of stitches is then worked in groups of six over the long bars of the preceding row, and the thread again brought, by overcasting, to the left side. The third and succeeding rows are then worked until the space is filled. When carefully done, the alternating filled and open spaces appear as little oblongs regularly placed. This stitch may be worked from side to side without overcasting the thread back to the left side after each row, but great care must be taken to get the loops or bars even and of equal length.

Somewhat more elaborate is the network shown in Fig. 62. The thread is fastened as usual at the upper left corner of the space. Two close Spanish net stitches are worked. A space just equal to that required for five close Spanish net stitches is left without stitches; then two more close Spanish net stitches are worked. This is continued to the end of the row. The working thread is then overcast once through each of the small loops between the pairs of Spanish net stitches, and several times over the long loop or bar. The

25

second row consists of groups of five Spanish net stitches worked over each long loop or bar. The thread is again overcast to the left side, and the third row begun. This is like the first row, and is composed of pairs of Spanish net stitches worked over the loops between the

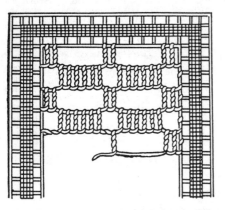

FIG. 62. SPANISH NET.

groups of five stitches of the second row. After each row the thread is overcast to the left side of the space, unless it is preferred to work alternately from left to right, and right to left. When finished, this network presents a broken check appearance, of oblongs and little squares, that is very effective.

In the Spanish Net stitch illustrated in Fig. 63 the thread is fastened in the corner and then carried by overcasting stitches along the edge of the braid about a quarter of an inch below. A net stitch is then placed in the upper braid about one-eighth of an inch from the corner. This is followed by two other net stitches set close together. A second group of three stitches is then worked at a distance from the first group equal to their own width. Between these groups of net stitches the thread is allowed

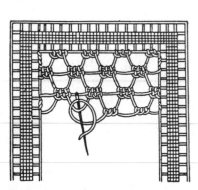

FIG. 63. SPANISH NET STITCH.

to fall in a long loop that reaches a very little below the level of the thread at its starting-point. These loose loops and groups of three net stitches are continued across the width of the space. The thread is then carried to the same distance from the corner as it is at the opposite side.

In every long loop of the first row three close buttonhole stitches are worked, and the intervening thread drawn quite tight in order to form a straight line across the space. The thread is then carried

along the edge of the braid for the same distance as before, and three buttonhole stitches are worked beneath the three of the former row, leaving the long loop between each group. These three stitches are not placed in the loops between the former groups of stitches, but the needle is thrust between the two threads of each buttonhole stitch. This brings the new row of stitches exactly beneath the other three above.

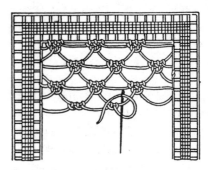

FIG. 64. SPANISH NET STITCH.

A variation of this stitch is shown in Fig. 64, and is obtained by working only two buttonhole stitches in each group of this row, and putting them on the loops between the buttonhole stitches of the former row.

Venetian or Point de Sorrento Stitch.

Point de Sorrento. — Line Stitch. — The Venetian stitches form one of the prettiest and most effective groups of stitches used. They are always less transparent than similar stitches without the straight line. When worked openly they present a cobwebby, misty effect that is decidedly beautiful.

The thread is fastened at the left-hand corner of the space to be filled, and a row of single net stitches is worked across the space at regular distances from each other, and far enough apart to

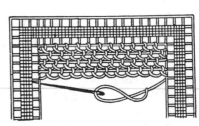

FIG. 65. LINE STITCH.

leave medium-sized loops between, as is shown in the illustration. When the end of the row is reached, the thread is carried down the side of the braid, until it is on a line with the lower edge of the loops. It is then carried across the space in a straight line, and passed through the edge of the braid at the left side. Care must be taken to have the thread tight enough to admit of no sagging, but not tight enough to draw the braid one particle from its place, and each successive line must be exactly parallel with its predecessors.

The second row of loops is then worked, and in

every stitch the needle is thrust through the loop above and back of the parallel thread, so that it is always held with the loop in the twist of the net stitch, and forms a part of the body of the lace.

A very novel effect is produced by missing some of the loops of the network, and in the next row working the same number of stitches in the loops so formed. The result is a series of open spaces in the close net work that is very odd. These open spaces may be placed at regular intervals over the entire network, or may be so spaced as to form a design. In Fig. 66 the first row is a series of close buttonhole stitches. The thread is then carried back to the opposite side, and a second row of buttonhole stitches over it is begun. Four of these stitches are placed, and the next four omitted. The following six are worked, and the next four omitted. The next four are worked. The next row is worked without any omissions. When the open spaces are reached,

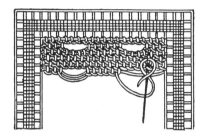

FIG. 66. VENETIAN STITCH.

the same number of stitches are worked in each as were omitted in the former row. In the following row the open space is left just between and below the two spaces of the upper row. Another complete row follows. The sixth row is a repetition of the second row.

Double Venetian or Cobweb Stitch.

One of the most beautiful and popular of all the lace stitches is the double Venetian. This is made in the same way as the single Venetian, except that, instead of a single buttonhole stitch in each loop, two are used. The two stitches aid each other in

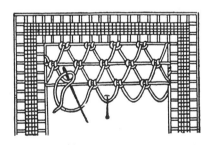

FIG. 67. COBWEB STITCH.

keeping the thread firmly in place, and make a very regular, substantial filling, that has a very fine lace-like appearance. The loop between the stitches is left loose and held in place with a pin as shown in the illustration.

This stitch may also be made with three buttonhole stitches in each loop, as shown in Fig. 68. Worked in this way the effect is decidedly close and solid, unless the loops are made sufficiently large to allow ample space for the three stitches.

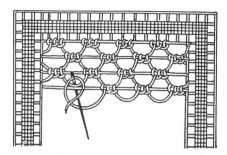

FIG. 68. VENETIAN STITCH.

Darned Figures on Venetian Background.

After a space has been filled with the plain, close Venetian stitch, it may be embellished in a variety of ways, and so made very effective and rich in appearance. With a fine linen floss, or other loosely twisted thread, pretty tufts or spots may be darned over two rows of the Venetian background. When worked at regular intervals, they add greatly to the richness of the work. Stars and trefoils in bullion stitch, buttonholed rings, and other fancy stitches may also be used.

When a very solid, cloth-like effect is desired, the Venetian stitch is worked with the net stitches very close together. Only sufficient room is left for the placing of the net stitch of the succeeding row. The straight thread aids also in producing an almost solid effect. This compact method of working this stitch is

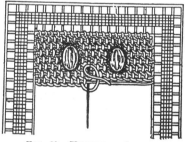

FIG. 69. VENETIAN STITCH.

seen most frequently in Venetian lace, where it is used as a filling for leaves, scrolls, and various parts of the design to be thrown out most effectively by the open background of Raleigh bars, or the even regular net ground.

Spider or Wheel Stitch.

This is a very rich and beautiful filling for large spaces. Beginning at the upper left corner, a diagonal line is laid across the space at an angle of forty-five degrees. The thread is then returned, but without twisting, to the first end of the diagonal line, so that the two threads form a double line lying close together but not crossing. At the selected distance a second line parallel with the first is laid across the space, and the thread as before returned to its beginning. This is repeated until the space is filled with rows of double parallel lines at equal distances apart.

Beginning near the upper right corner, a diagonal line is laid across the first lines at an angle of forty-five degrees, which makes it at right angles with the first series. The thread, on its return to the starting place, is passed three or four times around the threads of the intersections, which are not tied. This working thread must always pass under

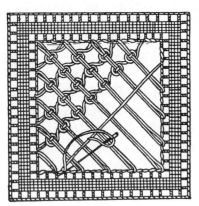

FIG. 70. SPIDER OR WHEEL STITCH.

the double threads of the completed series of parallel lines and over the single lines. When the wheel is sufficiently large, the thread is passed to the next intersection (which in case of the first row is the braid). A second thread is thrown across the space parallel with the first, and upon its return wheels are made at each intersection. This is continued until the space is filled.

Point de Bruxelles (Brussels Point).

A very pretty arrangement of Brussels point stitches is shown in Fig. 71. A row of net stitches is worked in pairs across the space. The two stitches are placed nearly but not quite close together. A space slightly greater than that occupied by these pairs of stitches is left between each group.

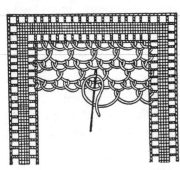

FIG. 71. POINT DE BRUXELLES.

The second row consists of a single net stitch placed between the pairs of net stitches forming the groups of the first row. The third row is formed by placing two net stitches in every loop formed by the distance between the single net stitches of the second row. The fourth row is like the second.

Point de Bruxelles.

Another variation of Brussels point is made by arranging the stitches in points or triangles. In Fig. 72, the first row consists of Brussels point stitches in an even, regular row just far enough apart from each other to easily accommodate the stitches of the next row. In the second row two stitches (or one loop) are omitted, and one net stitch worked in each of the next two loops. Two more stitches are omitted and followed by two net stitches, one placed in each of the two loops following. This arrangement of two stitches and an omitted loop is continued to the end of the row.

In the third row one net stitch

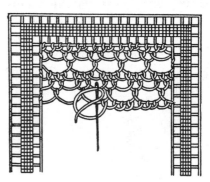

FIG. 72. POINT DE BRUXELLES.

is placed between each group of two net stitches of the second row. This row should be worked just loose enough to allow the long loops between the single net stitches to fall in very slightly curved lines. The fourth row is worked by placing three net stitches on each of the long loops of the fourth row. This is the first row of the second series of triangles, and is followed by a row of net stitches in pairs placed in the same way as in the second row, that is, two net stitches, one in each loop, and then the omission of one loop, followed by two more net stitches. The next row is the row of single net stitches that form the points of the triangle.

Larger triangles (see Fig. 73) are worked in the same way, except that the number of stitches in the triangles is increased, and consequently more rows are required to complete the figures.

The first row is the same continuous row of single net stitches as is shown in the smaller tri-

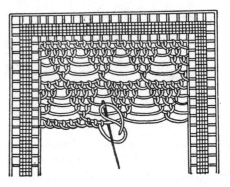

FIG. 73. POINT DE BRUXELLES.

28

angles. In the second row four stitches are worked and one loop omitted. In the third row three stitches are placed in the three loops of the preceding row, and so the work is continued till the points of the triangles are formed.

In this stitch, the loops being longer, they must be kept tight or straight enough to prevent the work from becoming too full for the space it occupies, and so the group of five stitches that begin each series or row of triangles may just fill the long loop prepared for them between the single stitches of the last row.

Many very pleasing results may be obtained by the arranging and grouping in various ways of Brussels net stitches. In Fig. 74 the first row consists of a series of single net stitches set at regular distances apart. The second row is the same until the middle loop is reached, when three net stitches instead of one are worked. The single net stitches are then continued to the end of the row. In the third row a group of three net stitches is placed in the first whole loop at the right of the

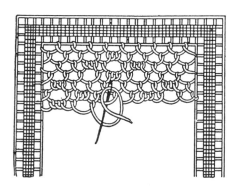

FIG. 74. POINT DE BRUXELLES.

group of three in the second row. A single net stitch is placed in the half loop at either side adjoining the group of three in the second row. In the next whole loop following, a second group of three stitches is worked. The fourth row is like the first. This brings the three net stitches exactly below those of the second row, and completes the quadrilateral or diamond-shaped pattern of the design.

In the fifth row two figures are to be begun, so the first group of three stitches is placed in the third whole loop preceding the close stitches of the row before, and another group of three is placed in the third whole loop following the close stitches of the previous row. These two groups of close stitches are the upper ends of the two quadrilateral figures to be worked. In the next row the close net stitches are, as in the third row, placed in the first whole loop at the right and at

the left of the group in the row above. The placing of the groups in the seventh row just beneath those of the fifth row completes this group of quadrilaterals.

Point de Bruxelles, "Pea" Stitch.

One of the prettiest of all arrangements of the Brussels net stitches is the one commonly known as the pea stitch, because of the open pea-shaped spaces formed by the method of the grouping of the stitches. This stitch is excellent for the filling in with networks of large spaces, and belongs to the design stitches, and not to the background stitches.

A row of Brussels net stitches is worked across the upper edge of the space to be filled. They should be placed regularly at even distances apart, and with room enough between them to place the stitches of the next row. In the second row a single net stitch is placed in the last loop of the first row. Two loops, which include three buttonhole stitches, are missed, and then one net stitch is worked in each of the next two loops. Two more loops are missed, and then two more net stitches are placed in the next two loops, and so the work is continued until the end of the row is reached. The third row is the row requiring care lest a mistake be made. Three net stitches are worked on the long loop of the previous row, and a single net stitch is placed between the two stitches between the long loops. The fourth row is like the second, and the fifth row is like the third. The long loop must be sufficiently loose to allow the curved appearance necessary to make the large openings nearly round.

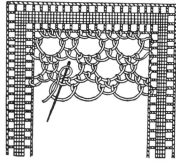

FIG. 75. POINT DE BRUXELLES, "PEA" STITCH.

Greek Net Stitch.

Greek net stitch is excellent for filling in large spaces, and is often used instead of spiders and twisted bars for the filling in of the background of lace patterns. As the beauty of this stitch lies in the perfection with which it is made, absolute regularity in the length and spacing of the stitches is necessary. The thread is fastened at the upper left corner of the space to be filled and carried down the side of the braid a distance nearly twice the length of a Spanish net stitch. At the same distance from the right of the corner, the needle is thrust into the edge of the

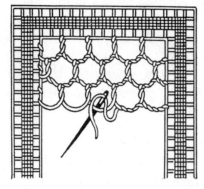

FIG. 76. GREEK NET STITCH.

braid, and a single Spanish net stitch worked. The thread is left loose or slack enough to fall in a rather long or decided loop equal in length to two of the Spanish net stitches. These single stitches are worked at regular distances across the entire length of the space, and are lifted up or shortened by a thrust of the needle in order to lengthen the loops and keep the net stitches the length of one side of the hexagon under construction. Each loop forms two sides of the hexagon. When the first row is completed, the thread is carried through the braid by a single stitch, and is overcast twice over each loop, evenly, and without drawing the loop out of its proper position, until the opposite side of the space is reached. The thread is then overcast along the edge of the braid the required distance, and a second row of single Spanish net stitches, like the first row, is made. The fourth row, like the second, consists of two overcasting stitches in each loop of the previous row.

Point Turque — Turkish Point.

The distinctive feature of Turkish point is the way in which the threads are knotted. When a diamond-shaped mesh is desired, the straight thread crossing the space may be omitted. When there is danger of not getting the loops exactly the same length, it is wise to thrust a pin through the pattern at the proper place, and pass the thread to form the loop around it. The experienced worker will doubtless find this use of the pin unnecessary. The thread is fastened in the upper left corner, and is carried down the edge of the braid a distance from the upper braid equal to the required length of the loops. The first stitch in the upper braid is placed a distance from the corner just half the width of the re-

quired diamond. As the triangles formed by each row of loops should be equilateral, each following stitch should be a distance from the preceding one equal to the length of one-half, or one side of the loop. To make the knot used in this stitch, the thread is laid in a circular loop just below the braid at the point of the proposed stitch. This loop is formed by passing the thread in a curve toward the right, extending close to the upper braid, and passing around toward the left and over the beginning of the loop. The needle is then thrust through the braid, under the upper curve of the loop, over the lower curve, and drawn up into a tight knot. This stitch, repeated at regular intervals between loops of exactly the same length, forms the first row. The thread is then attached

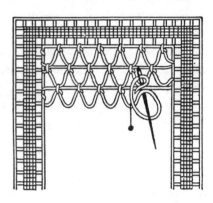

FIG. 77. POINT TURQUE.

to the braid at the right side, and carried down its edge to a point exactly in line with the middle of the loops. It is then carried across the space in a line parallel to the upper braid and attached to it. The next row is exactly like the first, the straight thread taking the place of the upper braid, and the needle at each stitch being passed under the loop above, under the straight thread, under the upper curve of the laid loop, over the lower curve of the loop, and drawn up into a tight knot.

Turkish Point.

Another form of Turkish point is usually made without the straight parallel lines thrown across the space. They may be made, if desired. The thread in this illustration is fastened in the upper right corner of the space. A short distance from

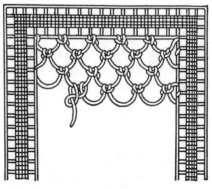

FIG. 78. POINT TURQUE.

30

the corner a plain buttonhole stitch is worked in the upper braid. Close to this a Turkish point stitch is worked. At the required distance from this pair of stitches a second pair is placed, with the loop between the two pairs long or slack. This is repeated to the end of the row. The thread is then carried down the side of the space, and the second row begun. This is like the first except that, being begun at the left side, the plain buttonhole stitch is each time at the left of the Turkish point stitch. This is continued until the second and each succeeding row is completed.

Point de Filet. Net Groundwork Stitch.

Point de Filet is an easy, speedy, and, at the same time, very beautiful stitch used for background or groundwork, instead of Brussels net. It is really an imitation of netting. It is worked diagonally across the space to be filled. The thread is fastened at the upper left corner of the space, and brought down the edge of the braid a distance equal to one side of the desired squares of the network. It is then carried across the left corner of the space, and fastened to the upper braid at a point equally distant from the corner. The loop must be just twice the length of the proposed square, so that when held in place by the knots of the next row it will form two sides of the corner square. The thread is then carried along the edge of the upper braid the same distance as before, and is fastened into the corner loop by means of a Turkish net stitch. The thread is then attached to the braid at the left the same distance as before from the adjoining fastening. These rows of diagonal loops, secured by knots of Turkish net stitch, are continued until the space is filled. The beauty of this stitch lies in its perfect accuracy. The vertical lines must be parallel and the horizontal lines must be parallel. This necessitates the making of all the loops of exactly the same length. To facil-

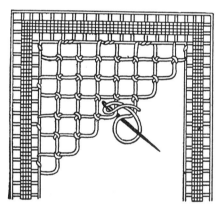

FIG. 79. POINT DE FILET.

itate this, pins may be stuck into the pattern at the right places, and the thread passed under them when the loops are being made. The work may be made still easier, if, before the stitch is begun, the space to be filled is checked off on the pattern with pen or pencil. Upon the finished network the various stitches used in netting, and many beautiful lace stitches, may be worked.

Point de Filet.

This stitch shows another method of tying the knot in point de filet. The thread is secured to the loops above it by a single Brussels net or buttonhole stitch. The needle is then passed under this buttonhole stitch or knot, over the working thread, under it, and drawn up tightly. This method very closely simulates netting and makes a good background for other stitches.

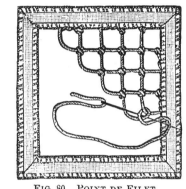

FIG. 80. POINT DE FILET.

Bruges Stitch.

The Bruges lace stitch is well adapted for the filling of large spaces, and may be used with or without the rosettes that give it its elaborate appearance.

Fasten the thread at the front left corner of the space, and overcast it along the edge of the nearer braid for the distance of one-fourth of an inch. Carry the thread across the space to the back or farther braid, and fasten it with a buttonhole stitch just one-fourth of an inch from the back left corner. Overcast the thread along the edge of the braid for a distance of one-sixteenth of an inch. About three-sixteenths of an inch from the back braid work a single buttonhole stitch over the long thread thrown across the space. Over the length of this buttonhole stitch place two other buttonhole stitches close together and extending toward the front end of the space.

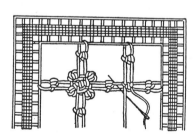

FIG. 81. BRUGES STITCH.

31

This is exactly as the "shells" in Point de Venise are made, only two instead of four stitches are used. This forms the "knots" that hold the parallel threads in place. One-half inch nearer the front braid work another buttonhole stitch over the long thread and fill its length as before with two buttonhole stitches. Repeat this at intervals of half an inch until the nearer or front braid is reached. Overcast the working thread along the edge of the braid for half an inch, and carry it across the space in a line parallel with the first thread. Fasten it with a single buttonhole stitch to the edge of the braid. If the thread is kept parallel, this point of attachment will be exactly half an inch from the first thread. Again carry the thread one-sixteenth of an inch to the right of the thread just fastened. At spaces exactly in line, from right to left, with the knots of the first row, make a new series of knots exactly one-half inch apart. Continue this until the entire space is filled with parallel lines from front to back of the space and at even distances apart, and whose knots form parallel rows from right to left across the space.

The work is now ready for the second series of parallel lines, which must intersect the first series exactly half way between the knots of the first rows. Turn the work around so that the finished lines extend from right to left instead of from front to back. This places the working of the second lines in the same position for working as were the first lines. Carry the working thread by overcasting stitches along the edge of the braids until a thread carried across the space will intersect the parallel lines *almost* half-way between the first two rows of knots. Fasten this thread with a buttonhole stitch and overcast it one-sixteenth of an inch along the edge of the braid. Work a buttonhole stitch over this long thread just as far from the intersection of the two lines as are the knots of the first lines. Over this buttonhole stitch work the two close buttonhole stitches that form the knot. Work another buttonhole stitch over the long thread exactly at the point of intersection. Work the two stitches that are to form the knot over both the buttonhole stitch and the threads of the finished line. Draw these stitches tight. This knot holds the two sets of lines together. At the proper place on the long thread (which is the same distance from the intersection as the other three knots surrounding it, and is also half-way between the first and second parallel lines already finished)

work another knot. Continue in this way until this line and the others which are necessary to fill the space are completed. This results in the open Bruges lace stitch, which is very effective when an open network is desired.

When it is decided to have the rosettes at the intersections, they are worked as each intersection is reached. The work is exactly as above until the knot which ties the intersecting threads has been worked (see Fig. 81). Around this knot the working thread is woven two or three times, by passing it over and under the surrounding threads in the manner of making a spider, as shown by the position of the needle in Fig. 81. This weaving being completed, the work of making the knots that form the rosette is begun at the space to the left of the long thread. In this right angle between the front and left-hand threads two buttonhole stitches, not too tight, are worked over the last threads of the spider. The needle is then thrust through the spider from beneath the work at the next angle, between the left hand and back threads, and two more buttonhole stitches are worked. This is repeated in the third and fourth angles. The needle is then thrust through the spider from beneath near the long thread, and the rosette is completed. The knot just between this and the next point of intersection is worked, and then the knot that ties the next crossing threads is made and the next rosette begun. This is continued until a rosette adorns each intersection throughout the space. A variation of this stitch may be obtained by surrounding the centre with a spider, but omitting the outer knots.

Point d'Angleterre.

This ground network is excellent for large spaces. The thread is fastened at the upper

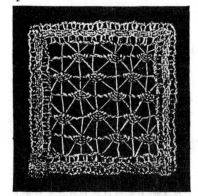

FIG. 82. POINT D'ANGLETERRE.

left corner, and carried along the upper braid the required distances for one check or square of the network. It is then carried across the space to the opposite side and entered into the braid, always keeping the working thread perfectly parallel to the edge of the left braid. The working thread is then overcast along the edge of the front braid, a distance equal to the distance between the first thread and the left braid. It is then carried to the upper or back braid and attached, forming another parallel line. These threads are continued across the space, all equally distant, and all parallel. Similar parallel threads are then laid across the space from right to left, and form a network of little perfect squares. The thread is next carried in diagonal lines from the end of each alternate parallel thread crossing the squares from right to left, and from left to right, and completing the network.

The thread is fastened in the upper left corner and carried along the left braid to the first horizontal parallel threads. This is overcast, and when the first vertical parallel thread is reached, the needle is passed back of both threads, thus securing the back one in the twist. At the first meeting of the four lines a half wheel is woven in an over and under darning stitch. The thread is then overcast in the same way to the next meeting of four threads, and a second half spider or wheel is worked. This is continued across this and each succeeding row until the space is filled.

Point d'Angleterre Rosette Stitch.

The thread is fastened at the upper left corner and overcast along the edge of the upper braid the required distance. It is then carried across the space to the lower or front edge of the braid and entered into it, making the thread so stretched across the space parallel with the left braid. The working thread is then overcast along the

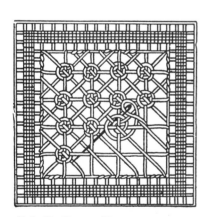

FIG. 83. POINT D'ANGLETERRE.

edge of the front braid a distance equal to that between the left braid and the first placed thread. A second thread parallel to the first is then laid across the space, and is followed by other equally distant parallel threads until the right side of the space is reached. Similar parallel threads are then carried across the braid from right to left, over

and under, and at right angles to the first series. The thread is then fastened to the left braid at the middle of the second square from the upper left corner. It is carried across the space diagonally to the upper right corner of the second upper square from the upper left corner, and crosses at the meeting of the horizontal and vertical lines. It is then carried one square to the right and again brought across the space in a line parallel with the first diagonal line. These parallel diagonal lines are continued across the entire space. The thread is then fastened to the right braid at the lower corner of the second square from the back right corner and carried to the upper left corner of that small square, where it makes the seventh ray diverging from that point. These threads are not tied together, but the needle is passed over and under the seven rays in several circles to form a wheel. Then the needle is passed from under that side of the wheel having the seventh ray and through the last circle of the thread of the wheel at the opposite side. This supplies the eighth ray by the fastening of the thread into the braid at the upper left corner of the little square thus entered. The thread is overcast along the braid to the upper right corner of the square to the left, crossed diagonally to its lower right corner, and a second wheel made. This diagonal line is continued across to the right side of the space and another wheel made at the next intersection of threads. The making of these diagonal lines and the wheels at the intersections is continued until the network is filled.

Hour-glasses.

Figure 84 shows still another arrangement of darning over the network described in No. 82. In

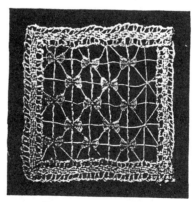

FIG. 84. HOUR-GLASSES.

this pattern two fans form little vertical hourglasses. The thread is fastened to the upper left corner, carried along the left braid, and overcast along the first horizontal parallel line to the first meeting of the parallel and diagonal lines of the network.

If preferred, these connecting threads may be fastened at their point of meeting by a single buttonhole stitch. The three upper threads are then covered with a woven fan and the thread carried back through the weaving to the centre. The lower three threads are then covered with a second woven fan and the thread again carried to the centre. The overcasting of the horizontal parallel thread is then continued till the location for the next pair of fans is reached. This is continued until all the double fans are worked.

Net with Rosette Stitch.

For this exceedingly beautiful net work the Penelope canvas, used for tapestry work, is imitated.

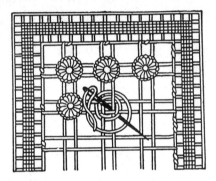

FIG. 85. NET WITH ROSETTE STITCH.

The thread is fastened at the upper right corner of the space and overcast along the edge of the right braid a distance equal to one side of the required larger square of the network. It is then carried to the left braid in a line parallel to the upper braid, attached to the braid, and overcast one stitch along its edge. It is again carried to the right side in a line parallel to the former one, and then overcast along the braid the length of the larger square. A second pair of parallel threads is passed across the space, and this is continued until the entire space is covered at regular intervals with these pairs of parallel threads.

The thread is then overcast along the front edge of the braid a distance equal to one side of the larger squares and woven under the lower and over the upper thread of each pair of horizontal lines. It is then overcast one stitch along the edge of the braid and returned to the lower edge by passing under the upper and over the lower threads. This alternates the weaving.

Upon this pretty network the rings are made. The thread is woven several times around the small squares and closely buttonholed. The thicker the foundation of circling threads and the more raised the buttonholing upon it, the more effective will be the result. At the completion of each buttonholed ring the thread is securely fastened and then cut. This makes each little ring independent of the others.

Greek Crosses.

The network for this filling stitch of little Greek crosses is the same as for the half spiders or wheels.

FIG. 86. GREEK CROSSES.

When the network is completed, the thread is fastened at the upper left corner and overcast to the first horizontal parallel line. This thread is overcast to the first meeting of four threads, securing the vertical thread in the overcasting. From the centre of this group of four threads, or eight radii, the thread is passed over and under the middle and left upper threads, forming a little fan. The needle is then passed through this fan to the centre, and a second fan woven over the middle and lower left threads. The third fan covers the middle and right front threads, and the fourth covers the remaining two threads. From the outer end of this last fan the thread is overcast to the next group of threads to be woven. A Greek cross of fans is thus made at every intersection of the vertical and diagonal lines of the network.

Point de Reprise.

The network for Point de Reprise may be prepared in either of two ways. In the first way

FIG. 87. POINT DE REPRISE.

horizontal parallel lines are carried across the space at even distances apart. The thread is then attached to the left braid at the left end of the upper line, and is then entered into the upper braid at one-half that distance from the upper left corner. It is then passed under the upper parallel line and again entered into the upper braid at a distance equal to the distance between the upper thread and the upper braid. This is continued across the space and makes equilateral enclosures. At the completion of the first row of enclosed triangles the thread is at the right end of the upper line. It is then passed under the second line and back to the first, passing under both the first thread and the thread looped around it at that point. It is again passed under the second thread and back to the first, forming the equilateral triangles of the second row. This is continued row by row until the entire space is laid off in a canvas-like network.

The second method of preparing this network is simpler. The parallel horizontal lines are laid as before. A series of diagonal parallel lines the same distance apart as are the horizontal lines are then woven over and under the first lines, across the space from the upper and right sides to the left and lower sides, crossing the horizontal lines at an angle of sixty degrees. A second series of diagonal lines is then woven in the same way and at the same angle from the upper and left sides to the right and lower sides. This completes the network of equilateral triangles.

These triangles are then covered with cones of darning. The thread is attached to the point or apex of the triangle to be covered, and the thread is passed over and under the foundation threads forming the sides of the triangle until the space is filled. It is then passed under the threads at the corner (which form the apex of another triangle) and carried down the side of the adjoining triangle to its apex. The darning of this triangle is accomplished and the work continued until the remaining triangles are covered.

Another method of covering the triangles consists of the use of buttonhole stitches. The thread is attached to the apex of the triangle. Two close buttonhole stitches are worked over the right foundation thread of the triangle. Then two are worked over the left side. In this way the working thread passes from one side to the other of the triangle after every second buttonhole stitch until the triangle is filled.

Combination and Miscellaneous Stitches.

Combination Stitches.

 IGURE 88 illustrates several stitches applied to different shaped spaces. In the leaf-shaped space marked A the stitch is worked as folows:

Fasten the thread at the upper right corner of the braid. Make a loop across the space and fasten the thread to the left side. Overcast one stitch along the edge of the braid and work seven buttonhole stitches into the loop. Attach the thread to the braid again and overcast two stitches along the edge. The third and fourth rows are Brussels net stitches. In the third row the stitch is taken in the fourth stitch of the group of seven. The fifth row is like the second.

For Fig. 88 B: Fasten the thread to the braid at the upper left corner. Carry the thread across to right side of the space, leaving the thread loose so as to form a loop. Overcast one stitch along the edge of the braid and stretch the thread back from right to left, keeping it perfectly straight. Overcast two stitches down on the braid, and work four buttonhole stitches into the loop and over the straight thread. The fourth row is an open network where the buttonhole stitches are taken between each group of the four close stitches. The fifth row is Brussels net stitches, and the sixth row is like the third.

BULLION STITCH USED FOR BACKGROUND.

35

Point de Valenciennes.

Point de Valenciennes is another form of diamond stitch (see Fig. 88 C). The thread is fastened at the upper left corner of the space and carried down the braid at the left side of the space, a distance slightly more than one buttonhole stitch. Near, but not close to, the corner a row of eight close buttonhole stitches is worked into the upper braid. A space equal to three buttonhole stitches is omitted and a second row of eight stitches is worked. This is continued across the space.

The thread is again carried down the edge of the braid at the right, and a buttonhole stitch is placed in the loop between the second and third stitches from the right of the first row. This is followed by a single close buttonhole stitch in each of the next four loops of the group of eight stitches. The result is five close buttonhole stitches worked in the middle loops of the row above, and leaves the two end stitches at either side to extend beyond the five below. Into the loop between the groups of eight two close buttonhole stitches are worked. Five more stitches are placed below the next group of eight, and are followed by the two stitches on the long loop between the groups. This is continued across the space. The third row consists of two buttonhole stitches placed in the two middle loops of each group of five stitches of the row above, and five stitches placed below the groups of two stitches. These groups of five are formed by placing two close buttonhole stitches close to the first stitch of the group of two above. One stitch is placed on the loop between them, and two close to the second of the two stitches. The fourth row consists of groups of eight stitches placed below the groups of five of the row above. The fifth row is like the second, and the sixth is like the third. This arrangement of stitches forms broad, flattened diamonds, and is suitable for filling large spaces. Another variation of this stitch is shown in Fig. 89.

Combination of Brussels Net.

The stitches shown in Fig. 88 D may be used for wide or narrow spaces by increasing or decreasing the length of the long loops, or, in filling large spaces, the width may consist of alternate rows of the short and the long loops.

The thread is fastened in the upper left corner, and one buttonhole stitch is worked into the upper braid one-third of the distance across the space. Two close buttonhole stitches are worked in the middle of the space. This is followed by a second single buttonhole stitch equally distant from the first. The thread is then carried to the braid and fastened. The second row is worked from right to left, and consists of six or more close buttonhole stitches worked on the long loop, completely filling it. Two close buttonhole stitches are worked on each of the small loops, and the second long loop is covered with six close buttonhole stitches. The third row is like the first, and the fourth row is like the second.

The stitch illustrated in Fig. 88 E, like the preceding one, is suitable for broad or narrow spaces, and is used for wide spaces by repeating the stripes of the pattern.

FIG. 88. COMBINATION STITCHES.

The thread is fastened at the upper left corner and carried down the side of the braid one stitch. A short distance from the corner a single stitch is worked into the upper braid. Space for two stitches is omitted, and a second single stitch is worked. These stitches should occupy one-third the distance across the space. At the end of the second third of the space a single buttonhole stitch is worked, making a long loop extending across the middle of the space. Space for two stitches is then omitted, and a second single buttonhole stitch is worked. The thread is then fastened into the braid at the right and carried down one stitch. A single buttonhole stitch is worked into the short loop between the two buttonhole stitches above. Six or more stitches are then placed upon the long loop, filling it. A single stitch is then worked in the left short loop, and the thread attached to the braid. The third row is like the first, and the fourth is like the second.

The stitch used in Fig. 88 F is the Petit Point de Venise and is described on page 19.

Fans.

Woven fans make a very effective filling (see Fig. 88). They may be made singly, in pairs, or in trios. They may be built like hour-glasses or like Greek crosses. They may have few or many foundation threads. They may have graduated points or they may have a flat end.

To make a trio of fans as illustrated, the thread is fastened at the point of the braid selected for the base of the fans. It is then carried to a point on the opposite side of the space a distance to the left of the centre just half the width of the middle section or division of the fan. The thread is passed through the braid and overcast back to the base of the design, always overcasting from the worker.

COMBINATION OF FANS WITH OTHER STITCHES.

To do this the pattern is so held that the base is the farthest point in the space from the worker. This way of overcasting ensures a better twist to the threads. When the first thread is brought back to the base it is entered into the braid at the same point from whence it started. It is again carried across the space and entered into the braid at a point just as far from the centre to the right as the first one was to the left. This is overcast to the base. The third thread is entered into the braid a sufficient distance to the left of the left thread already in place and overcast to the base. The opposite right thread is then placed in the same way. The remaining distance at the left of the threads already in place is now filled with four similar threads, all overcast, equally distant and meeting at the base. The right side of the space is filled in the same way. The weaving of the fans should be begun with a long thread and at the base. The middle fan may be woven first. The thread is carried over and under the four threads alternately in a weaving or darning stitch and must be drawn just tight enough to keep the twisted threads in place, to preserve a sharp point at the base and an even edge at the sides of the fan. When it is desired to begin the pointing, the two outer threads are dropped and the weaving is continued over and under the two middle threads. When the weaving is completed the needle is passed from the point to the base of the fan through its centre, or between the threads of the weaving, so as to be invisible. The thread is now in place to begin the weaving of the second fan. This and the third one are then woven.

Woven Rays.

Woven rays form another showy effect (see Fig. 88). The base is naturally the converging part of the space, and the outer edge of the group of rays is the side of the larger curve. Each ray has its own base and these bases are located close together, so that each, though a part of the whole central effect, is complete in itself.

The desired positions of the outer ends of the rays are selected at equal distances from each other, and three threads for each ray, diverging from its own base, are put in position and overcast. These are covered with the over and under darning or weaving stitch throughout their entire length. All weaving must begin at the narrowest point in the design to be woven. The thread may be attached to the braid at the completion of each ray or may be carried back through the interior of the first ray and overcast to the base of the next.

Diamond Stitch.

When a rich, showy effect is desired, there is no stitch more appropriate for large spaces than the diamond stitch. The beauty of this stitch lies in its regularity, and in keeping the diamonds sufficiently close together and in straight rows. The thread is fastened in the upper left corner and brought down the side of the braid the distance of one buttonhole stitch. At a short distance from the corner, equal to the space necessary for two stitches, a group of four buttonhole stitches is worked. These stitches must be just far enough apart to admit, on the second row, one similar stitch on each of the loops between them. These four stitches being completed, a space equal to three stitches is omitted, and one buttonhole stitch worked. Another space of equal length is followed by a second group of four stitches. These groups of four stitches and single stitches are continued across the space to be filled, great care being taken to keep the spaces between them of equal length. The first row being completed, the thread is carried down the edge of the braid one stitch.

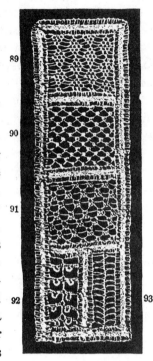

FIG. 89, DIAMOND. FIGS. 90 and 91, POINT DE SORRENTO. FIG. 92, BULLION INSERTION. FIG. 93, KNOTTED RUSSIAN STITCH.

In the second row begins the alternate increasing and decreasing of the diamonds started by the first row. One buttonhole stitch is placed on the long loop, close to the right side of the single stitch of the first row. This is followed by a second single stitch placed close to the left side of this same single stitch of the first row. Into each of the three loops between the four stitches of the next group of the first row, a single buttonhole stitch is worked. In working the first of these three stitches care must be taken to make the loop between this and the group of two stitches already made of the same length as the loops between the groups of the first row. All the long loops through-

out the work must be of the same length. At each side of the next single stitch of the first row a single buttonhole stitch is worked, both stitches being kept close together. Into the loops between the following group of four stitches three buttonhole stitches are worked. This is continued to the end of the row. The third row also consists of groups of two and three stitches. Into the loops between the stitches of the groups of three in the second row two buttonhole stitches are worked, and this is followed by three stitches below the following group of two. The first stitch is placed on the long loop close to the left of the two stitches; the second stitch is placed between them, and the third on the long loop close to the right of the two stitches. Two stitches placed one in each of the two loops of the next group are followed by three stitches below the next group of two. This is continued to the end of the row.

The fourth row, like the first, consists of groups of four and single stitches. Below the group of three stitches, at the left of the space, four stitches are worked, care as usual being taken to keep the first and last of this group, which are worked on the long loops, close to the other two. This group of four stitches is followed by a single stitch between the two stitches of the row above, and completes the half diamond begun at the first row. The next group of four stitches follows, and so the work is continued to the end of the row.

The fifth row begins the new diamonds below the half diamonds begun at the first row, and diminishes the diamonds begun by the single stitch of the first row. Two stitches are placed below the single stitch, and are followed by a group of three stitches below the group of four of the preceding row. This is continued to the end of the row, and is followed by the sixth row, which is composed of groups of three stitches below the groups of two stitches of the preceding row, and groups of two stitches below the groups of three. The seventh row is like the first, and completes the alternate whole diamonds begun by the first row.

Point de Sorrento.

Point de Sorrento is very similar in appearance to the double net stitch. The method of placing the stitches makes it exceedingly firm, and, where an open network is desired, this stitch is very practical and beautiful. The thread is fastened at the upper left corner of the space, and at equal listances two buttonhole stitches are worked close together. The first is a plain buttonhole stitch worked into the edge of the braid; the second stitch is placed close to the first, and is passed through it. To do this, the needle is thrust both through the braid and between the two threads that form the sides of the loop of the first stitch, and is then drawn up close in a buttonhole stitch. At the proper distance from this pair of stitches a second buttonhole stitch is worked in the edge of the braid. Into the loop of this stitch a second buttonhole stitch is made as before, and so the work is continued to the end of the row. The rows are all alike, each pair of buttonhole stitches being placed on the loop between the two pairs of stitches above, and each pair of stitches is interlocked.

Point de Sorrento.

This stitch should not be worked too closely. The more open it is, the more showy the effect. In making buttonhole stitches from right to left, the thread must be thrown or carried around into position for each stitch, while, when working from left to right, the thread naturally falls into position, and the extra movement of placing it is obviated. Hence, it is always well when beginning a stitch, to so regulate your work that the rows having most buttonhole stitches may be worked from left to right. Because of this it is best to fasten the thread for this arrangement of Point de Sorrento at the upper right corner of the space. At equal distances, and somewhat far apart, groups of two buttonhole stitches, placed rather close together, are worked across the space. The thread is then carried down the edge of the braid the length of a buttonhole stitch, and the second row of stitches begun. On the loop between each pair of loose buttonhole stitches of the first row a group of three close buttonhole stitches is worked. The third row is like the first, that is, two rather loose buttonhole stitches are worked on each of the long loops between the groups of three stitches of the second row. The fourth row is like the second.

Bullion Insertion.

When a heavy, showy insertion is desired, Fig. 92 is excellent. The thread is fastened at the upper right corner and carried down the edge of the braid a distance equal to the length of a Spanish net stitch. Into the upper braid, at the middle

of the space, a single Spanish net stitch is worked, and the thread attached to the edge of the braid at the left side, a distance from the corner equal to the distance the thread at the right side is from the right corner. The thread is then carried one stitch down the edge of the braid, and on the left long loop three close buttonhole stitches are worked. Through the loop between the second and third stitch, the needle is thrust for about half its length, and the thread is wound around its point ten or twelve times. The thumb is then placed upon the coil of threads, the needle drawn through, and the thread pulled up so closely that the coil assumes a circular shape.

This is followed by three more buttonhole stitches on the long loop. The long loop at the right of the Spanish net stitch is covered exactly as was the left loop. The three close buttonhole stitches are followed by the picot in bullion stitch and completed by three more close buttonhole stitches. The third row, like the first, consists of a single Spanish net stitch placed on the loop in the middle of the second row. The fourth row is like the second. When the space to be filled is rather wide, a greater number of buttonhole stitches will be necessary on either side of the bullion stitch.

Knotted Russian Stitch.

Knotted Russian stitch is a very neat, easily made, and effective insertion. The space is first filled with plain or twisted Russian stitches made at even distances apart, and somewhat close together. When the space is curved, care must be taken to regularly place the stitches on the outer curve at an equally greater distance apart. This ensures regularity in the result. When the space is entirely filled, the thread is passed to the middle of one end of the space, and a close buttonhole knot is tied tightly on each single thread of the insertion as it passes the middle of the space.

The stitch is especially useful for filling leaf or other long narrow space.

Point Lace proper was not produced to any extent before 1620, whatever may be said to the contrary. Reticella work of the seventeenth century is the nearest approach to it, but still retains traces of plaiting and Genoa stitch, which were never employed in real point. Point proper became the dress lace *par excellence* under Louis XIV.

Combination Stitches.

Another pretty network is made by a combination of Brussels net and Spanish net stitches, as shown in Fig. 94. The thread is fastened at the upper right corner of the space to be filled, and a row of Brussels net stitches worked at regular intervals. The thread is then fastened to the edge of the braid at the left of the space, and overcast along its edge a distance equal to the length of the Spanish net stitches. Into the first loop of the Brussels net stitches of the first row a single Brussels net stitch is worked. Into the second loop three Spanish net stitches are placed. The third loop holds one Brussels net stitch, and into the fourth are worked three Spanish net stitches. This is continued to the end of the row. The third row is like the first — a row of open Brussels net stitches. The first stitch is placed at the right of the three Spanish net stitches of the row above, and the second is placed in the loop at their left. In this way the trio of Spanish net stitches is considered as one stitch, and the loop between the first and second Brussels net stitch encloses them all. The next Brussels net stitch is placed in the next loop of the row above, and the work so continued to the end of the row. The fourth row is composed like the second, of single Brussels net and trios of Spanish net alternating. The Spanish net stitches are placed in the loops below or under the single Brussels net stitches of the second row. This results in the Spanish net stitches occurring in diagonal lines across the network, and is more graceful and artistic than if placed in lines under each other.

One of the prettiest of networks is composed of alternating rows of Spanish net and Brussels net stitches, as shown in Fig. 95. The thread is fastened at the upper left corner, and a row of single Spanish net stitches is worked at regular intervals far enough apart to admit on the loop between them five or six close Brussels net stitches. When the opposite edge of the space is reached, the thread is attached to the braid, and overcast along its edge the required distance. A group of five or six close Brussels net (or buttonhole) stitches is worked over each loop between the Spanish net stitches. These Brussels net stitches must be evenly and closely worked and there should be enough of them to fill closely, but not crowd, the loop upon which they are worked. Each loop of the first row of stitches is filled in this way with the Brussels net stitches.

The thread, upon reaching the end of the row, is again attached to the braid and overcast along its edge the length of the Spanish net stitch. The third row consists of the single Spanish net stitches placed on the little loop between the groups of Brussels net stitches and just under the stitches of the first row. The fourth row is like the second. When completed the network shows a pattern of open squares, with the heavy lines of Brussels net stitches reaching in parallel lines from right to left across the space, and the lighter Spanish net stitches forming parallel lines at right angles to the Brussels net stitches.

A similar but less geometrical network is made wholly of Brussels net stitches (see Fig. 96).

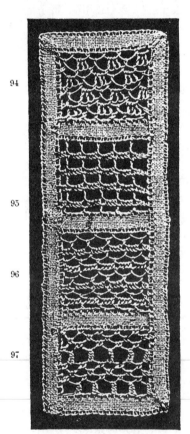

94

95

96

97

The thread is fastened at the upper left corner and a row of open Brussels net stitches is worked at regular intervals across the space. The thread is then overcast along the edge of the braid as usual, and a second row of open Brussels net is worked into the loops of the first row, one stitch being placed in each loop. The third row is the close row. Into each loop of the second row is worked five or six close Brussels net, or buttonhole. stitches. There should always be the same number of these stitches in each loop, and there should be enough of them worked closely together to nearly fill the loop. A row of open Brussels net stitches is next worked, one stitch being placed on each loop between the groups of close buttonhole stitches of the third row. The next, or fifth row, is like the second, and the sixth row is like the third.

An exceedingly delicate and attractive stitch is shown in Fig. 97. The thread is attached to the upper right corner of the space, and three rows of

40

open double net stitch are worked. To accomplish this, two buttonhole stitches close together, and drawn rather tight, are worked at regular intervals into the braid across the space. The second row consists of two close buttonhole stitches worked into each loop of the first row. The third row is like the second. At the completion of the third row the thread is overcast along the edge of the braid for a distance about equal to that necessary for a Spanish net stitch. A single buttonhole stitch is worked into the first loop of the preceding row, and left somewhat loose. Point de Venise or side stitches are now used. A close buttonhole stitch is worked over the single net stitch close to the loop to which it is attached. This is drawn closely and followed by three or four more side stitches set closely together. There must be enough of them to so fill the long loop that there is only a slight downward curve to that part left uncovered, and into which the next row must be worked. When the first group of side, or Point de Venise, stitches is completed, another single long Brussels net stitch is worked into the next loop, and this in turn is filled with the same number of side stitches as were used to cover the first long stitch. This is continued to the end of the row, and is followed by three rows of double net stitch, after which the row of long Point de Venise stitches is repeated. This is continued in the same order of three rows of double net and one of Point de Venise, until the space is filled.

Combination Stitch.

In Fig. 98 is shown a pretty combination of Brussels net, Spanish net, and Venetian stitches. The thread is fastened at the upper left corner, and two rows of Brussels net stitches are worked. The thread is then overcast one stitch lower, along the edge of the braid, at the side of the space, and then carried in a straight line across the width of the space and through the braid at the right side, just below the second row of Brussels net stitches. Two close buttonhole stitches are worked over each loop, and in every instance over the straight thread also. This makes the Venetian stitch. The thread is again carried across the space, and a second row of Venetian stitch worked. In this row one buttonhole stitch is worked between each of the stitches of the row above. The working thread is then overcast along the edge of the braid the required distance, and a Spanish net stitch is worked between every

other stitch of the row above. The working thread is then carried twice across the space, and should lie in close parallel lines just at the edge of the loops

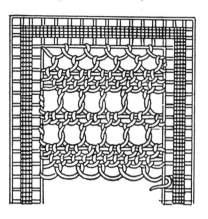

FIG. 98. COMBINATION STITCH.
Brussels Net, Spanish Net, and Venetian Stitch.

of the row of Spanish net stitches. A row of Venetian stitch is then worked over these two threads, and the the loops of the Spanish net stitches by placing two Brussels net stitches on each loop between the Spanish net stitches. If preferred, only one straight thread may be carried across the space for this row of Venetian stitch. A second row of Spanish net stitches is then worked, one between every two Venetian stitches of the row above. This places the Spanish net stitches exactly under the Spanish net stitches already worked in the row above. Two rows of Venetian stitch are next made and the space is completed by the working of two rows of Brussels net.

A very pretty effect is produced by alternating two or three rows of Venetian stitch with one of Spanish net throughout the space. In this case the Brussels net stitches at the beginning of the network are omitted, and the network should begin with one row of Spanish net stitches and should also end with a row of the same.

Combination Stitch.

Another pretty stitch is shown in Fig. 99. The thread is fastened at the upper right corner and a row of open Brussels net stitches is worked across the space. The thread is overcast along the edge of the left braid a distance equal to the Brussels net stitches. A single net stitch is worked in the first loop of the row above. This is repeated at the second loop. Into this second stitch a group of four close buttonhole stitches is worked. The thread is passed through the middle of the net stitch and drawn up in a rather close buttonhole stitch. Three other similar stitches are worked close together in the same opening. A single Brussels net stitch is placed in the next loop of

41

the row above, and this single Brussels net stitch is followed by another cluster of four stitches within the single Brussels net stitch placed upon the next loop. This is repeated to the end of the row. The third row is like the first and the fourth is like the second.

FIG. 99. COMBINATION STITCH.

Combination Stitch.

This exceedingly beautiful stitch was taken from a piece of lace made in Ireland. The thread is fastened at the upper left corner. It is then held by the thumb, or secured by a pin, in a long loop, and at a distance to the right of the corner equal to one side or half of this long loop five close buttonhole stitches are worked. A second long loop is secured, and five more buttonhole stitches worked. The third long loop follows. These loops must be of exactly the same length. The thread is entered into the braid at the left, and overcast along its edge a distance equal to two buttonhole stitches. Into the first long loop two close buttonhole stitches are worked. These are held in place by the thumb, and two more stitches are placed on the middle loops of the five stitches of the row above. Two more stitches are then placed on the next long loop, and are followed by two on the middle loops of the next group of five stitches. This is continued to the end of the row.

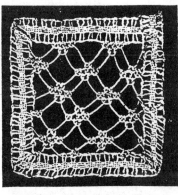

FIG. 100. COMBINATION STITCH.

The thread is again attached to the braid, and two close stitches are worked at the left of the first group of two stitches of the second row. One stitch is placed upon the loop between the group of two stitches, and close to them at the right two more close stitches are worked. This makes a row of five close buttonhole stitches under the two of

the row above. The thread is not carried up to the next group of two stitches, but a long loop is secured, as in the first row, and five close buttonhole stitches are worked below the group of two stitches, swinging on the long loop of the row above. Another long loop is secured, and five more close stitches worked. This is continued across the space. The fourth row is like the second, and the fifth is like the third.

Combination Stitch.

Fig. 101 is a very showy stitch, suitable for heavy, sumptuous effects. The thread is fastened at the upper right corner, and a row of large loops is made by working single Brussels net stitches rather far apart, and making the loops between somewhat long. The thread is attached to the left braid and carried down one stitch. A row of ten close buttonhole stitches is then worked upon the first loop, filling it smoothly but not tightly. The left thumb is then placed firmly upon the second loop to prevent its being pulled out of shape, and to bring the stitches close up to the edge of the braid in order to preserve the scalloped effect. The first buttonhole stitch is then placed upon the second loop and drawn up very tightly to the braid. The other nine stitches are then worked, and the thumb placed upon the third loop, ready to assist in the shaping of the next curve. This is continued to the end of the row. The third row is like the first, except that the buttonhole stitches are placed between the fifth and sixth stitches of each group of the row above. The fourth row is like the second.

FIG. 101. COMBINATION STITCH.

Connected Needle-made Picots.

Connected needle-made picots make a pretty finish for the edge of a piece of lace, and are made after the lace is completed. The thread is attached to the edge of the braid with a buttonhole stitch. Over this another buttonhole stitch, called a seed or side stitch, is worked. This is the little

42

Point de Venise stitch already given. The thread is then carried over and through the loop, and is tied with a second buttonhole knot or side stitch. This is repeated at regular intervals, leaving the loops between of uniform size, and long enough to fall in graceful curves.

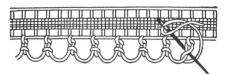
FIG. 102. CONNECTED PICOTS

Isolated Needle-made Picots.

Another method of finishing the edge of lace is to make isolated picots. These have open pendent loops, and resemble to some extent the machine-made edges. The thread is attached to the braid with a buttonhole stitch. A pin is then thrust through the pattern, upon which the lace is still basted, at a point indicating the required length of the picot. The thread is then passed around this pin from right to left, and crossed again to the right, forming an oval loop. It is then passed across the loop again, and the needle thrust behind the buttonhole stitch and the end of the loop over the thread that again crosses the picot, and drawn up in a tight buttonhole knot. At the required distance from the first picot, a second buttonhole stitch is made into the edge of the braid, and the thread between this and the finished picot is drawn up to form a straight line parallel with the braid. The pin is again placed in position, and the second picot is made and tied with a buttonhole knot, as be-

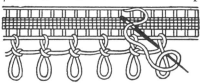
FIG. 103. ISOLATED PICOTS

fore. These picots are repeated at regular intervals along the edge of the braid.

English Wheel Insertion.

One of the prettiest and most adaptable stitches for narrow spaces, straight or curved, is the English wheel insertion shown in Fig. 104. When the space is straight the bars must be equally distant and parallel, but when it is curved the arrangement of the bars must be regulated by the curve, closer together at the inner side and farther apart at the outer side, always evenly spaced and always maintaining the direction of radii from a common centre. The making of these bars is shown in Fig. 5.

When they are completed a thread is carried from one end to the other of the space (tied at each cross bar when the space is a curve) and then twisted back upon itself, and a web woven at each intersection with the cross bars. These webs are made to keep their shape by passing the thread through instead of over and under the twists of the bars.

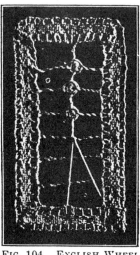
FIG. 104. ENGLISH WHEEL INSERTION.

Half-Bar Insertion.

For an easy effective insertion stitch the half-bar insertion, Fig. 105, is excellent. The thread is secured at one end of the space, and carried in a plain Russian or buttonhole stitch into the braid at one side of the space. A single stitch is taken into the braid just below the first one to keep the work from curling. Close buttonhole stitches are then worked upon the bar thus formed, the number depending upon the width of the space and the effect desired. Two or three may be sufficient or the bar may be covered with them almost to the centre of the space.

Buttonholed Russian Stitch.

Plain Russian stitch, Fig. 24, is the foundation for the insertion shown in Fig. 106. After the entire space has been filled in with the plain Russian stitches the working thread is secured to the middle of one of the end braids and the desired number of buttonhole stitches worked over each of the foundation stitches. The illustration shows this insertion with a decoration of one, and of three stitches over each foundation stitch.

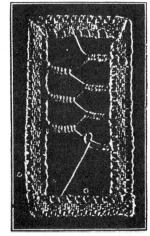
FIG. 105. HALF-BAR INSERTION.

43

Knotted Russian Stitch.

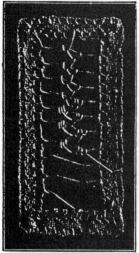

FIG. 106. BUTTONHOLED RUSSIAN STITCH.

Another variation of plain Russian stitch is shown in Fig. 107. After the space has been filled with the plain Russian stitch, spaced far enough apart to give the desired effect, the working thread is overcast in a close even coil along each diagonal line of the Russian stitch almost to the edge of the braid. Here a single buttonhole stitch is taken around the entire foundation stitch and drawn up into a tight knot. These knots must be maintained at an even distance from the braid.

Twisted Brussels Net.

A very effective variation of Brussels net is shown in Fig. 108 and is excellent where a uniform stitch a little heavier than the single Brussels net is desired. A single row of buttonhole stitches is worked into the braid from left to right at uniform distances apart across the space. The working thread is then carried back to the left by passing

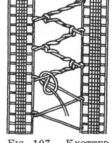

FIG. 107. KNOTTED RUSSIAN STITCH.

it once into each loop between the buttonhole stitches. The second row consists of a single buttonhole stitch worked into each loop of the first row, passing each time between the loop and the overcasting thread. This is continued until the space is filled.

Point de Venise Bars.

An original adaptation of Point de Venise or shell stitch (Figs. 43-45), is shown in Fig. 109 and is a very useful arrangement for the many little spaces that require

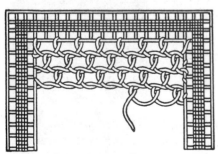

FIG. 108. TWISTED BRUSSELS NET.

a little more than the plain twisted bar. As is clearly shown in the illustration, the thread is carried across the space, entered into the braid and a single stitch below taken. A single buttonhole stitch is worked across this bar at the point selected for the shell. Across this and at right angles to it a second buttonhole stitch is worked and is succeeded

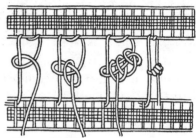

FIG. 109. POINT DE VENISE BARS.

by two or three more, each worked between its predecessor and the bar. The working thread is then entered into the right braid, completing a bar parallel with the first one.

A Knotted Edge.

Many times a hand-made edge is preferred to the little machine-made braid that is usually used to edge needle-made laces. A single row of Point de Venise shells makes a beautiful border, but when something less time-consuming is desired the pretty little edge shown in Fig. 110 is excellent. The work always proceeds towards the right. The thread is secured to the braid, brought to the right and curled back to the left in a loop which is held down by the left thumb. The needle is then entered into the edge of the braid, passed through the loop and drawn up into a rather close knot. The spacing of these stitches must be uniform except in turning curves, where the stitches must be set more closely together, but the connecting loops left sufficiently loose to allow the work to lie flat.

Brussels Net.

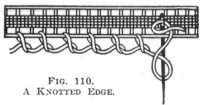

FIG. 110. A KNOTTED EDGE.

A very attractive open network is shown in Fig. 111. A row of rather closely spaced buttonhole stitches is worked entirely across the space. In the second row a single buttonhole stitch is worked at regular intervals into the previous row enclosing each time six of these stitches. In the third row four rather loose buttonhole stitches are worked, or hung upon, each of these

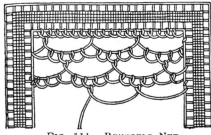

FIG. 111. BRUSSELS NET.

large loops. The fourth row consists, like the second, of the large loops placed each time on the middle loop of the group of stitches above. The fifth row, like the third, consists of four buttonhole stitches on each of the loops above.

Diamond Stitch in Brussels Net.

The diamond arrangement of Brussels net stitches shown in Fig. 112 is very showy and effective for filling in large spaces. Groups of six rather closely set buttonhole stitches are worked at regular intervals with a space between the groups equal to the width of one of them, and with the loop kept long. The second row consists of a group of three buttonhole stitches worked into the three

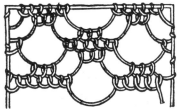

FIG. 112. DIAMOND STITCH IN BRUSSELS NET.

middle loops of each group above and three buttonhole stitches worked on each long loop. The third row is composed of groups of six stitches worked under each three of the preceding row, two stitches to the left of the first stitch above, one on each loop and two to the right of the last or third stitch. The loops between the groups are left long and the next row, like the second, consists of three stitches in each long loop and three below the groups of six.

Spanish and Brussels Net.

Figure 113 is a simple combination of Spanish and Brussels net stitches. As the Spanish net

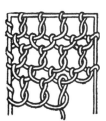

FIG. 113. SPANISH AND BRUSSELS NET.

stitch is always worked more easily from left to right the work is begun at the left and a single row of the Spanish net stitches (Fig. 58), worked across the space. The second row consists of a single Brussels net stitch (Fig. 38), worked in the loop between each of the Spanish net stitches

above. These rows of Spanish and Brussels net are worked alternately until the space is filled.

Ringed Raleigh Bars.

This is one of the richest and most beautiful of the lace stitches and will greatly add to the beauty of any piece of lace in which it is used; see Fig. 114. The rings may be the fine

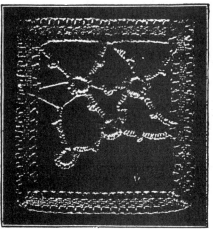

FIG. 114. RINGED RALEIGH BARS.

Flemish machine-made variety or they may be made by the worker. When this is preferred the foundation of each ring is prepared by winding the thread a sufficient number of times around a ring gauge (Fig. 1) or other suitable cylindrical implement. These windings are held together by overcasting them with the working thread, and the rings, not yet buttonholed, are basted into position on the pattern. They may be spaced regularly and the bars arranged in a geometrical design as shown in the illustration or they may be placed without regard to design and the bars put in according to necessity—either effect is good. After the rings have all been securely fastened to the pattern by means of a sufficient number of stitches to hold them securely the bars are worked. The thread is fastened to the braid at any point, carried across to the nearest ring, and through it, and the bar so made covered closely with buttonhole stitches back to the braid. At any given point in the bar a picot may be placed. This is made by working three close button-hole stitches be-tween the

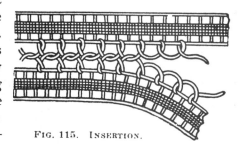

FIG. 115. INSERTION.

last two on the bar and then continuing the buttonholing until the bar is completed. Often these bars must be from ring to ring and not

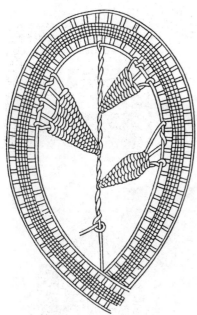

FIG. 116. LEAF INSERTION.

connect with the braid at all, and often the working thread must be carried along the ring until the desired location for the beginning of the next bar is located. The last time the thread enters the ring a covering of close buttonhole stitches is worked over it.

Insertion.

A pretty little insertion is shown in Fig. 115. A single buttonhole stitch is worked at regular intervals into the braid along the entire length of one side of the space. The same treatment is given to the other side with the stitches placed exactly opposite those of the first and the working thread passed once through each loop of the opposite row. Should the space vary in width at any point the connecting of the two sides may be omitted, and after the buttonholing of the second side has been completed the working thread carried down the open space and a single buttonhole stitch worked into each loop alternately. This results in a plain Russian stitch worked into the loops instead of into the braids. In wider separations of the braid the working thread may be passed once into each free loop and the whole drawn up and either buttonholed closely or overcast several times more, and then, if the

size of the enclosed space warrants, filled in with any preferred web or stitch.

Leaf Insertion.

A very handsome insertion is shown in Fig. 116 and may be varied as the ingenuity of the worker may dictate. The working thread is secured at one end of the space, carried across, entered into the braid, and overcast or twisted back to the point at which the first leaf is to be worked. Here it is secured by a single buttonhole knot left just loose enough to admit the needle, and from this point is entered into the braid on the side and at the location at which the lower end of the leaf is to be. It is then overcast one or two stitches along the braid and carried back into the buttonhole knot in the midrib. From here it is again entered into the braid to form the third rib of the leaf, overcast back to and passed through the buttonhole knot. This results in two single and one twisted bar upon which to work the leaf and brings the working thread to the starting point of the weaving, which is done by passing

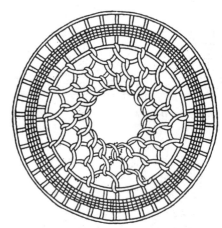

FIG. 118. NET STITCH IN CIRCLES.

it over and under the bars or ribs until a leaf of solid weaving of sufficient size has been made. The working thread is then passed down through the weaving to the base of the leaf and the overcasting of the midrib then continued by twisting to the point on the opposite side of the space at which the second leaf is to be located.

The illustration shows three varieties of these leaves. The first is the simple three-ribbed fan. The second is a fan of five ribs and may be varied and given a pointed or leaf shape by dropping the two outside bars when the leaf is half finished and continuing the weaving over the three inner ones only. A third leaf is shown, which is given the curved leaf shape by slightly drawing the last few rows of weaving to conform to the shape desired.

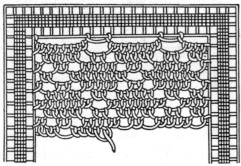

FIG. 117. DIAMOND DESIGN IN BRUSSELS NET.

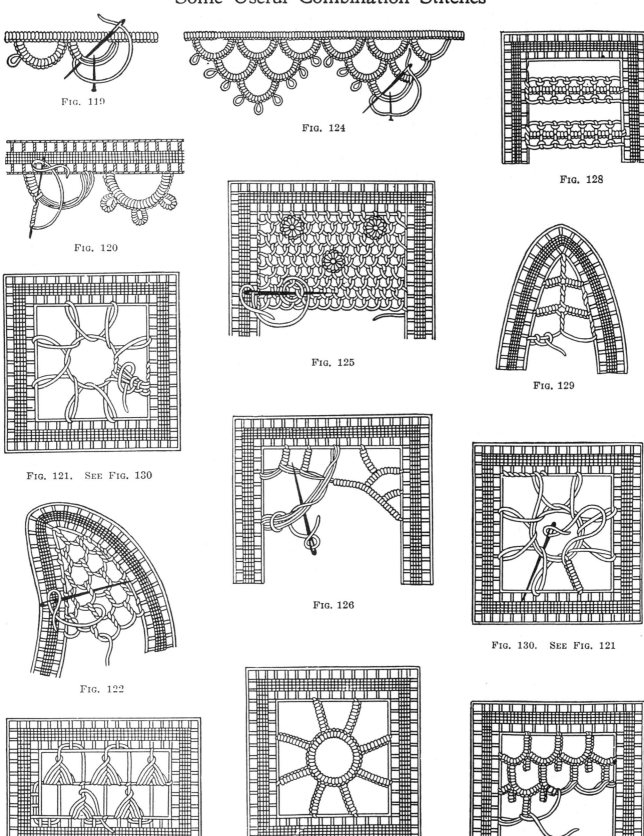

FIG. 119

FIG. 124

FIG. 128

FIG. 120

FIG. 125

FIG. 129

FIG. 121. SEE FIG. 130

FIG. 126

FIG. 130. SEE FIG. 121

FIG. 122

FIG. 123

FIG. 127

FIG. 131

Diamond Design in Brussels Net.

Figure 117 shows another very handsome diamond design in Brussels net. The first row consists of single buttonhole stitches worked at intervals so spaced as to make a loop long enough to accommodate eight rather closely set buttonhole stitches, and these long loops separated by a shorter loop. In the second row eight buttonhole stitches are worked on each of the long loops, but no stitches on the shorter loop. In the third row five stitches are worked under the groups of eight and two stitches on the loop connecting the groups of eight. In the fourth row two stitches are worked under the groups of five and five stitches under the groups of two. This is done by making two stitches to the left, one on the loop between and two to the right of each group of two.

In the fifth row eight stitches are worked under each group of five—two to the left, one between each of the five and two to the right of the group of five. No stitches are worked between the groups of two. The sixth row is like the third and the seventh like the fourth, and the work so continued until the space is filled.

Net Stitch in Circles.

In large circular spaces where webs or radiating stitches are not desired the size of the space may be reduced by a circling of Brussels or Spanish net stitches worked at regular intervals into the braid and drawn up by overcasting the thread once into each loop; see Fig. 118. If once circling the space does not reduce its size sufficiently any desired number of successive circlings may be worked, each stitch into the loop above. As the size of the space grows less the stitches will become smaller and closer together, and sometimes it is advisable to omit every alternate loop of the preceding row. The final circling of stitches may be merely gathered into a circle or may be further finished by a covering of close buttonhole stitches, or a little web be woven across the opening. The working thread is then overcast from circle to circle back to its starting place in the braid and fastened. Medallions of this kind can often be used as inserts for dainty lingerie, and for such a purpose the centre space could be filled with a woven wheel. Such medallions would be pretty in the corners of a handkerchief.

Net or Appliqué Lace.

MANY beautiful effects may be obtained by combining lace braids and stitches with net. Marie Antoinette is a net or appliqué lace on a larger scale. The same methods may be employed to make the finest and daintiest of filmy laces. In the former, cords, rings, and various heavy showy braids are used to produce flowers and foliage, bow-knots and scroll effects. In the finer laces the regular point and honiton lace braids are used.

The net is basted carefully and smoothly on the stamped pattern. Much of the perfection of the finished work depends upon the neatness and exactness of this part of the work. The lines of the pattern will be clearly seen through the net, and over these the braid is basted.

Where the net underneath is to be cut away the edge of the braid must be fastened to the net with close buttonhole stitches of fine thread. The inner curves must be fastened into position, and, if the net is not to be cut away, these edges must also be buttonholed to the foundation.

With care the drawing of the inner curves into position may be done with the buttonholing. When this can be done the overcasting is unnecessary.

When the net is not to be cut away the braid may be attached by close overcasting stitches. A row of braid almost always outlines the edge of the lace. This is also buttonholed firmly to the net and has an edge of purling overcast to its outer edge. Occasionally the braid is omitted and the purling alone is buttonholed to the net. This makes a lighter but less durable finish for the lace. The various lace stitches are then worked into the design of the braid. In honiton appliqué the braid medallions are buttonholed into position according to the pattern, which is usually a floral design. The stems of the various leaves and flowers are sometimes worked in tent stitch and sometimes are darned into the meshes of the net. The centres of flowers are usually finished with needle-made buttonholed rings.

Instead of the lace stitches used in the point

appliqué, a very pretty effect is obtained by filling in the spaces with darned net stitches.

Dots may be sprinkled over the net by weaving the thread around and around a selected mesh of the net. Another way is to work bird's-eye stitches, using several threads. These bird's-eye stitches make pretty leaves and sprays when worked in the design of the lace. A third method of dotting the net is to work little buttonholed rings at regular intervals, or the tiny rings used in point lace may be added if the net is heavy.

When the lace is finished it is removed from the pattern, and the net to be removed from under medallions and lace stitches is carefully cut away. The edge is also cut close to the buttonholing that holds the lace edge in position. The lace is then pressed under a damp cloth.

How to Wash Lace.

TO wash lace successfully, plenty of time and great care are necessary. There are instances where hurried work is followed by success, but the chances are against it. A Battenberg doily became soiled in the making, so the maker rubbed white soap on it, thrust it in a basin of hot water, and rubbed it vigorously between her hands, until all trace of soil was gone. She then pulled it out into shape, placed it between two towels, and rolled it up. When nearly dry, she ironed it, still between the towels, and, strange to say, that doily showed no bad results from its rough treatment.

A still more remarkable instance was that of a fine modern point lace handkerchief, made with thread No. 1000. This handkerchief accidentally went with the family linen to the washerwoman. The adventures it went through at her hands will forever remain a mystery, but when it reached home it was white and clean, ironed and folded, and none the worse for its experiences.

But these cases are rare, and are also unfortunate, as they lead to carelessness in accomplishing a work that should receive the most careful treatment. Sometimes all that is necessary to clean a piece of lace is to lay it between two sheets of white or blue paper, first sprinkling it well with powdered magnesia. Then place it between the leaves of a book, and allow it to remain for several days. When the magnesia is shaken out, the lace will be found to be very greatly improved. Lace placed between sheets of blue paper will keep white longer than when placed between white paper, or laid away in a box.

When actually washing is necessary, take a glass bottle whose body is as nearly cylindrical as possible. Half fill this with sand or water, to prevent the water when boiling from tossing the bottle about too violently in the kettle. Very carefully wind the lace around this bottle, and cover it with a layer of cheesecloth or muslin. A still better way is to baste the lace smoothly and exactly on a piece of cheesecloth, then wind it securely around the bottle, and cover the whole with another layer of the cheesecloth.

Into a granite saucepan put some cold water, a small piece of soap, and, if the lace is very dirty, a pinch of salt. Into this plunge the lace-wound bottle, and let the water come to a boil. As the water gets dirty, pour it off, and replace with more cold water and soap. Continue this treatment until the boiling water remains perfectly clean. Then remove the bottle, and plunge into a basin of clean cold water, and rinse thoroughly. Allow the lace to remain on the bottle until it is dry, then remove it and separate from the cheesecloth.

When real lace has become stained or greasy from wear, place it in a bath of pure olive oil, and allow it to remain for several hours or even a day or two. This gives to the lace the softness of texture it possessed when new. After this is accomplished, wind the lace on the bottle, and proceed with the boiling, as already described.

When the lace is too large to wind around a bottle, baste it evenly and securely to a piece of cheesecloth, with small stitches in parallel lines across the surface of the lace. Baste another piece of cheesecloth over it, and boil in a series of waters. After the rinsing, which must be accomplished by pressing and squeezing, but never by wringing, pin the cloth upon which the lace is basted smoothly to a sheet stretched in curtain frames; or, if this is impossible, to a sheet stretched and pinned over a carpet. Allow the lace to dry, and then remove from the sheet and from the two layers of cheesecloth.

If you wish the lace starched, dissolve a sufficient amount of starch in cold water. Boil half of it, and, when partly cool, stir in the uncooked half and add cold water until the mass is of the consistency of cream. Into this dip the lace, and gently squeeze out the extra amount. Lay the lace in a flat mass in the left hand, and spat it thoroughly with the right until the starch is well worked in. Repeat the process if desired, and roll the lace in a towel and leave for some hours.

To color lace a cream shade add a few drops of black coffee to the starch. To make the lace a greenish hue use a little cold tea.

Machine laces may be ironed directly upon their surfaces. First carefully and smoothly pull all the picots into place and see that the lace is exactly in its original shape; iron until dry. Then pull the lace along its entire length between the fingers from the footing or engrêlure to the opposite edge. Pass the iron again over its length. The pulling relieves the lace of the stiff, starched effect, and makes it as pliable as new lace.

To iron unstarched lace place it right side down upon a pad or ironing-board covered with several thicknesses of white flannel. Over this spread carefully a damp cloth and press with a hot iron until this cloth is thoroughly dry. This is also the way to press newly made lace, and should be done as soon as the lace is removed from the pattern. A little white sugar added to the water in which this over-cloth is dampened will stiffen the lace, and is in some cases much better than starch. Another excellent method is to dampen a piece of new organdy or other white goods containing starch or dressing. Place this over the lace and iron till dry. This gives a crisp new appearance to the lace without making it at all suggestive of starch. Another method of washing lace is to soak it about fifteen minutes in a bowl of suds made of white soap and water. Pour this off and replace with a clean suds. Place the basin where the sun will shine upon it. Change the lather twice a day and let the rays of the sun restore the lace to its original whiteness. When it is clean rinse it in

several clear waters, pressing but never squeezing, and drop it in a dainty heap on a plate. Leave it here till it is only damp, not wet. Dissolve two lumps of white sugar in a pint of water, and into this drop the lace. Allow it to remain for about five minutes. Squeeze this sweetened water out and spread the lace smoothly upon the soft, flannel-covered ironing-table. Over it place a piece of white muslin and iron with a warm, not too hot, iron until it is dry. Remove the cloth, and, taking the lace in the hands, carefully manipulate with the fingers until the lace has been restored to its original shape. Then with a fine lace needle, which has no point to tear and split the delicate threads, carefully open and shape each picot.

Irish guipure and real point lace should be pinned out, not ironed. This is quite a task, and should be attempted only when the worker has ample time and is not liable to be interrupted. A large wooden drum or hoop of sufficient width is best, but if this is not to be had, a large circular box or a straight board may be used. Pad the outer surface of this drum on both sides and the ends of the board with several layers of white flannel, and, if preferred, cover this with a piece of white muslin stretched smoothly.

Lace must, of course, be damp when pinned, and then the pins will not tear the threads of the picots. Only a portion of the length should be removed from the damp cloth within which it is rolled. Should the lace, being pinned, become dry, dampen it with a wet cloth or sponge. First pin the footing or engrêlure down to the padded support, using plenty of pins placed close together. Spread the lace across its width smoothly over the support, and pin each picot separately by thrusting the pin through it and into the flannel support as if it were a cushion. The pins must be the exact size of the picots, as their size must keep the picots in their original shape. Leave the lace until it is thoroughly dry and then remove the pins. If the lace has a raised design, rub it gently on the wrong side with a lace awl.

EDITORS NOTE:

The above discussion on washing lace should be viewed for historic interest only. Time has demonstrated that many of the methods described are detrimental to the life of a piece which is intended to be preserved and will definitely cause more harm then good.

While some laces are far sturdier then others, caution should always be exercised in caring for any lace item. If in doubt, do nothing.

The following basic tips are intended primarily as establishing a method for preventing further harm from occuring to a lace not properly cared for:

1. Never store lace in any wood or ordinary cardboard container. 2. Never wrap lace in blue or any other color material. 3. Never use starch on lace. 4. Never iron directly on a piece of lace. 5. Never use brass or steel pins in lace. 6. Never use oil or any organic substance on lace. 7. Store lace only in an acid free box and wrap only in white acid free tissue. 8. If pinning, use only stainless steel pins.

Actual cleaning of lace should be done with caution. Laces, when wet, are heavy and if not properly handled will be damaged from their own weight. Actual methods will depend on the type and age of the work as well as the materials used.

If the reader is interested in pursuing this area the following book is suggested:

TEXTILES, HOME CARE AND CONSERVATION, Audie Hamilton (\$7.50 suggested retail). Available through this LACIS.

PATTERNS

The patterns illustrated in this appendix can be ordered, full size, from your dealer or from this publisher. Patterns are printed on heavy paper and can be used in accordance with instructions on page 1 of this book. Sizes noted are approximate and can vary slightly. Sizes of any pattern, other then that noted are available on special order. Many of the handkerchiefs and tie ends, for example, can be adapted, in this way, to curtain designs.

For individual pattern prices, refer to the letter following the pattern number which will correspond to the price listed below. Add $2.00 for postage and handling. All prices are subject to change.

A	$1.50	E	6.00
B	2.50	F	7.00
C	3.50	G	8.50
D	5.00	H	10.00

5527.0-G, 36"

5526.0-G, 36"

5524.0-G, 36"

5434.0-D 20"

5435.0-D, 17"

5441.0-B 8" x 13"

5441.1-A, 3.5"

5426.0-A, 5"

5395.0-C, 11"

5400.0-C, 13"

5403.0-A, 5"

5393.0-C, 11"

5399.0-C, 11"

5402.0-A, 5"

5396.0-C, 11"

5405.0-B, 11"

5421.0-B, 7"

5397.0-C, 11"

5404.0-C, 11"

5416.0-G, 36"

5387.0-A, 8"

5418.0-C, 17"

5433.0-F, 27"

5419.0-A, 8"

5438.0-D, 16"

5417.0-C, 12"

5422.0-D, 20"

5420.0-D, 19"

53

5407.0-A, 4"

5519.0-B, 10"

5223.0-D, 27"

5522.0-D, 19"

5520.0-B, 11"

5521.0-D, 25"

5406.0-A, 7"

5518.0-D, 18"

54

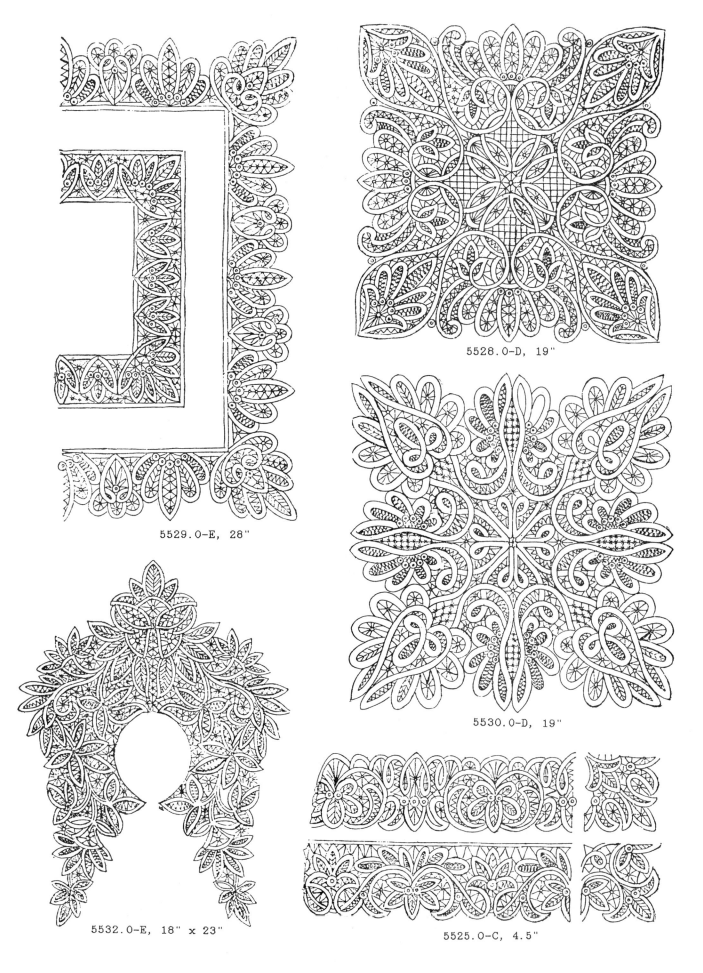

5529.0-E, 28"

5528.0-D, 19"

5530.0-D, 19"

5532.0-E, 18" x 23"

5525.0-C, 4.5"

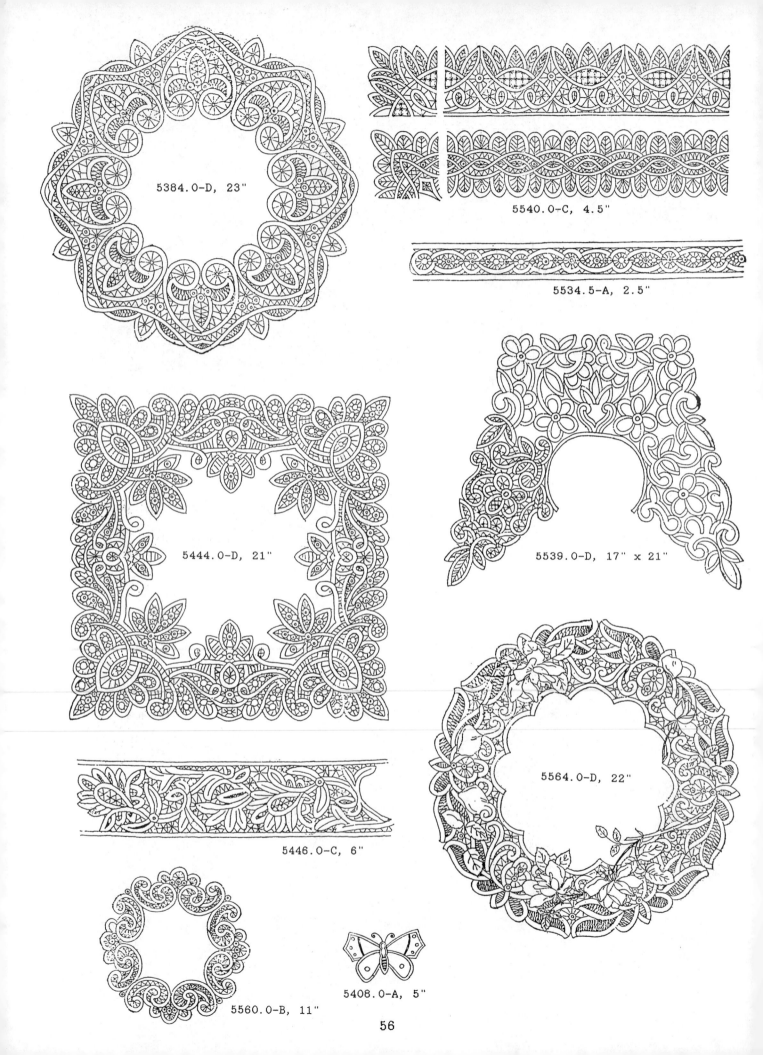

5384.0-D, 23"

5540.0-C, 4.5"

5534.5-A, 2.5"

5444.0-D, 21"

5539.0-D, 17" x 21"

5446.0-C, 6"

5564.0-D, 22"

5560.0-B, 11"

5408.0-A, 5"

56

5515.0-D, 4"

5517.0-A, 9"

5516.0-C, 11"

5512.0-D, 23"

5513.0-C, 11"

5514.0-C, 11"

5511.0-D, 23"
5511.5-F, 30"

57

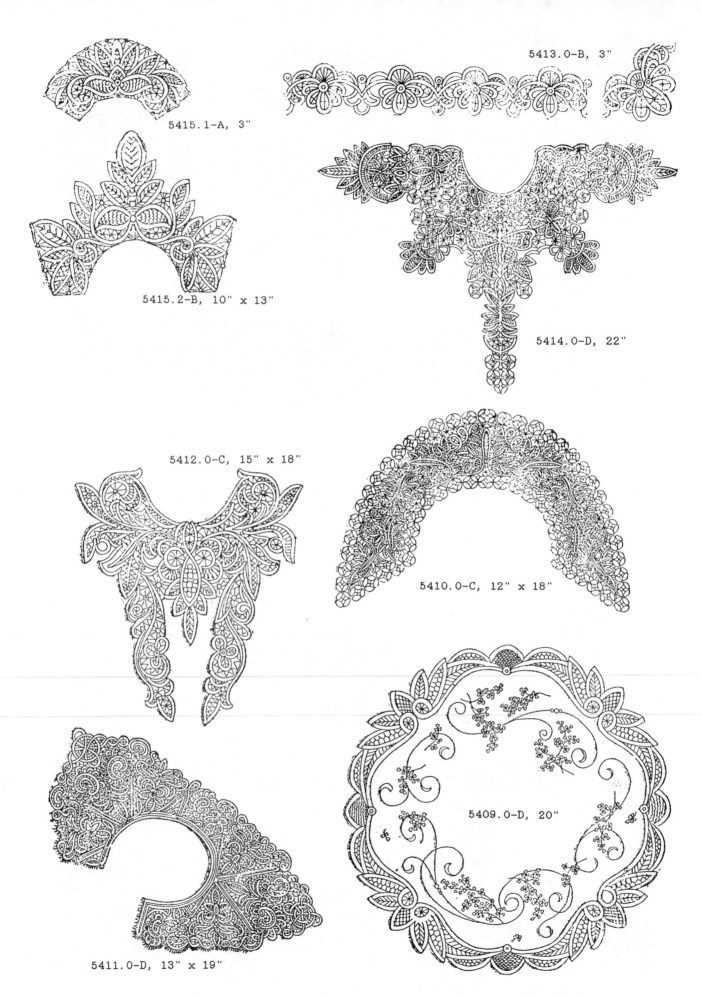

5415.1-A, 3"

5413.0-B, 3"

5415.2-B, 10" x 13"

5414.0-D, 22"

5412.0-C, 15" x 18"

5410.0-C, 12" x 18"

5409.0-D, 20"

5411.0-D, 13" x 19"

5431.0-E, 12"

5442.0-D, 23"

5425.0-C, 4"

5563.0-C, 11"

5423.0-B, 3.5"

5445.0-A, 6"

59

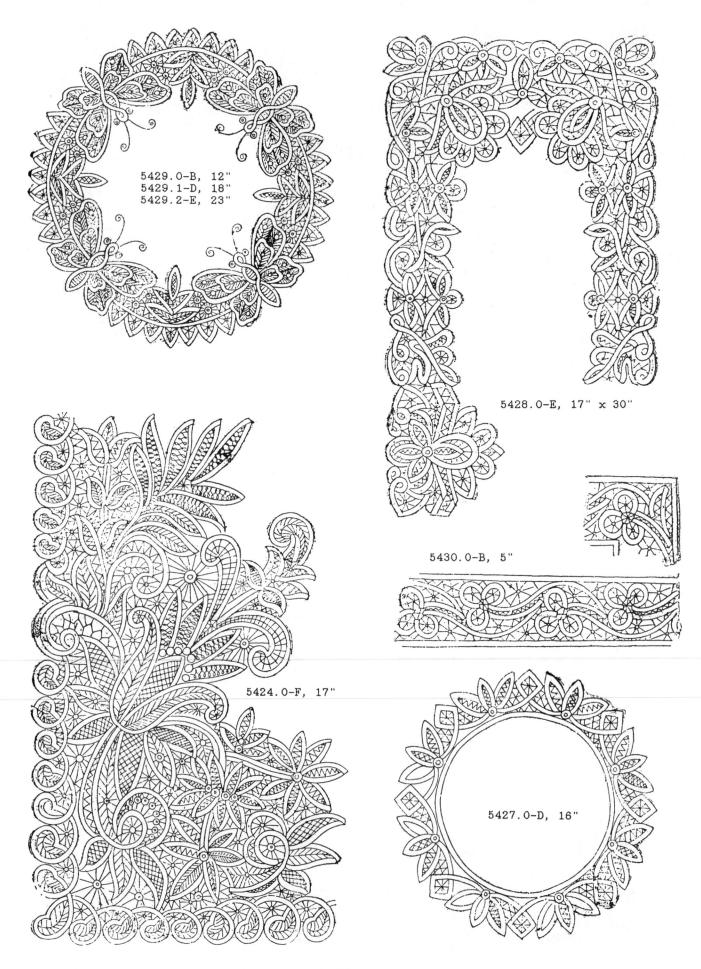

5429.0-B, 12"
5429.1-D, 18"
5429.2-E, 23"

5428.0-E, 17" x 30"

5430.0-B, 5"

5424.0-F, 17"

5427.0-D, 16"

5437.0-B, 8"

5439.0-B, 10"

5436.0-A, 5"

5451.0-B, 4.5"

5497.0-D, 16"

5542.0-C, 11"

5394.0-D, 9"

5509.0-A, 9"

5450.0-A, 8"

5448.0-A, 9"

5533.0-B, 11"

5535.0-H, 12"

5538.0-E, 30"

5541.0-F, 30"

5536.0-C, 18"

5534.0-F, 30"

5443.0-A, 3"

5398.0-A, 10"

5401.0-A, 5"

5388.0-C, 11"

5389.0-C, 11"

5390.0-C, 6"

5391.0-H, 28"

5383.0-E, 20" x 26"

5385..0-A, 7"

5392.0-G, 23"

5440.0-A, 6"

5573.0-A, 5"

5386.0-B, 10"

5531.0-B, 4"

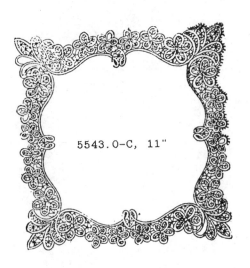

5543.0-C, 11"

5537.0-D, 4"

5449.0-B, 10"

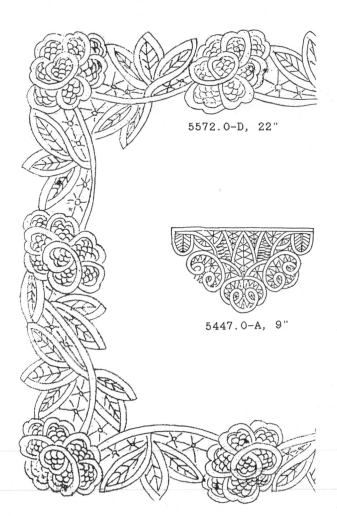

5572.0-D, 22"

5547.0-B, 10"

5447.0-A, 9"

5544.0-C, 11"

5571.0-B, 4"

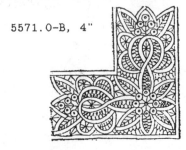

5548.0-A, 10"